MANNERS and MORALS of the 1920's

MANNERS
and MORALS
of the 1920's

A Survey of the Religious Press

by

Sister Mary Patrice Thaman,
C.PP.S.

GREENWOOD PRESS, PUBLISHERS
WESTPORT, CONNECTICUT

Library of Congress Cataloging in Publication Data

Thaman, Mary Patrice Sister.
  Manners and morals of the 1920's.

    Reprint of the ed. published by Bookman Associates,
New York.
    Bibliography: p.
    Includes index.
    1. United States--Moral conditions. 2. Journalism,
Religious. 3. United States--Social life and customs--
1918-1945. I. Title.
[HN90.M6T47 1977]   973.9   77-8129
ISBN 0-8371-9679-5

Copyright 1954, by Bookman Associates Inc.

Originally published in 1954 by Bookman Associates, Inc.,
New York.

Reprinted with the permission of Twayne Publishers (A
Division of G.K. Hall Corp.).

Reprinted in 1977 by Greenwood Press, Inc.

Library of Congress Catalog Card Number 77-8129

ISBN 0-8371-9679-5

Printed in the United States of America

TO MOTHER

Preface

The pitfalls in writing a work based on periodicals as a principal source are numerous, but well worth the risks to one who begins his task well-armed with confidence of rewarding results, well-shod for the devious amblings through mountains of magazines, and well-armored against the darts of criticism which are not infrequent in a work of this nature.

The intention to compile a study of this kind crystallized in a seminar conducted under the direction of Doctor Jasper W. Cross at Saint Louis University, in 1950. The role of religious periodical literature as a medium of public opinion in the field of history had been a favorite theme of speculation for some time. Hence, it was with a kind of headlong eagerness and a throbbing expectation that this work was begun.

The study has proved well worth every effort. It has shown religious leaders and spokesmen keenly alerted to the revolution in manners and morals during the 1920's, and would indicate that it is possible to glean from journals and magazines a picture of contemporary history with more than a fair degree of objectivity.

A work of this nature inevitably involves debts more numerous than those that can be acknowledged in a prefatory note. To all whose interest and aid have meant much to me, I give my assurance of gratitude.

Very special expressions of appreciation are due to Reverend Mother M. Borgia, C.PP.S., who graciously afforded me the time and opportunity necessary for this research. To Doctor Jasper W. Cross, for his unfailing encouragement, generous assistance, and helpful suggestions, I shall ever be grateful. A special word of thanks is also due to Reverend Gerard L. Poelker, who graciously accepted the tedious task of reading the manuscript.

It is hoped that this single volume may enable the reader to readily evaluate the opinion of the religious press on the changing manners and morals of the 1920's.

SMP

Contents

"Report uttered by the people is everywhere of great power."

Aeschylus—*Agamemnon*, 938.

CHAPTER I

Introducing Issues

John Macy, author and journalist, once said: "The American press is an accurate gauge of the American mind." Nor has he stood alone in his assertion. Charles Evans Hughes felt that "public opinion in a democracy wields the scepter," and Charles Dudley Warner would have us remember that "public opinion is stronger than the Legislatures, and nearly as strong as the Ten Commandments." But there has been a formidable array in the camp of the opposition.

Historians, by and large, have been perhaps too prone to write off all press material as inaccurate, unreliable, and sensational. It seems to be accepted as axiomatic that the more difficult material is to uncover, the more worthy it is of credence. In general, there has been a hesitation in accepting and in recognizing the value of the press. When citations from newspapers and periodicals are made, many authors sound their utterances in a semi-apologetic undertone.

Lucy M. Salmon has ably treated the problem in a work with the telling title of *The Newspaper and the Historian.* Her critical analysis is probably one of the best evaluations of the importance of the press to a study of history. She declares:

> For . . . the study of normal life the newspaper,—abnormal as it itself may seem with flaring headlines and blurred pages of illustrated advertisements, with all of its limitations, its inaccuracies, its unworthy representatives, its lack of proportion, its many temptations—not always resisted—to throw prismatic colors instead of the white light of truth on its accounts of the day, . . . still remains the most important single source the historian has at his command for the reconstruction of the life of the past. . . .[1]

The present work purports to be a historical study; hence, primary emphasis will be placed on what was actually said. Of course, there must be a background for the men who acted and spoke, had ideas and principles which determined their lives. This study will depend on periodicals as the principal sources because the particular objective was to determine the living, day-by-day attitude. Editors and writers contributing to the press are not necessarily the leaders of public opinion, but they are usually the most prominent in expressing their opinions. Hence, an examination of the editorial comments of Catholic, Protestant,[2] and Jewish journalists in the decade of the 1920's should enable one to discover how the most vocal groups among these denominations reacted to certain manners and morals of that period.

Books, no doubt, would reveal a more thorough, better-considered opinion, and more deliberate comment, but an indisputable advantage of using a popular source is that it will better express the thought of the average man and of larger groups.

Obviously, for purely physical reasons, if for no others, it was impossible to examine all the publications of the denominational groups. Hence, screening was necessary.

One factor determining the choice of the particular publications here used was their contemporary prominence as indicated by the frequency of allusions made to them or of quotations cited from them. But the selections were made primarily because these magazines are most officially representative, as far as that is possible, within groups having varying degrees of autonomy—of the respective religious bodies.[3]

The manners and morals under focus in this study are those which were rather generally discussed by all religious groups, and apparently considered of importance also by profane authors writing on the decade. The ten year period fairly teems with items such as Peace Conferences, League of Nations, Prohibition, Scandals in Government, Immigration Laws, Vatican Relations, K. K. K., Spiritualism, Modernism, and while every one of these matters received passing notice—and in some instances much more comment—in the editorial columns of our religious journals, it is the intention of this work to limit itself only to manners and morals which consistently occupied a place of primacy of interest in our periodicals. Here, again, limits had to be set up. Manners such as fashions, fads, movies, automobiles, professional sports, and morals such as birth control, companionate marriage, divorce, and crime will be our concern.

It is not the purpose of this work to condemn or to praise the various opinions. A simple, though undoubtedly legitimate, procedure is to trace, during a period of time, the expressions of thought about manners and morals which emanate from persons and groups formally professing a particular religious creed. Such expressions, of course, may be placed in perspective against the intellectual climate of time and place so that significant comparisons may be made.

This study applies this simple historical and comparative approach.

"I know where there is more wisdom than is found in Napoleon, Voltaire, or all the ministers present and to come—in public opinion."

Talleyrand—Chamber of Peers, 1821.

CHAPTER II

A Look at the Literature

For the sake of perspective, but at the risk of wending a way made dull by mere factual information, it seemed necessary to include a chapter that would present a survey of the periodical literature used in this study.

Three magazines, *The Baptist*, *The Word and Way*, and *The Watchman-Examiner* were selected to speak for Baptist opinion. The Baptists, as is generally known, divided into a Northern Convention and a Southern Convention. In 1923 there were 425 associations, 631 churches, and 1,267,721 members in the Northern group. The Southern section counted 986 associations, 27,634 churches, and 3,444,383 members. These figures seemed to warrant the examination of a periodical speaking for the North and one for the South.

The Baptist, a weekly magazine published in Chicago, is entitled the official newspaper of the Northern Baptist Convention, and is generally recognized as such by its contemporaries.[1] However, from its own editorial columns, it becomes apparent that it is not an official paper in any restricted sense. It "is the concrete expression of the will of the denomination . . .[2] and is also "a denominational organ. It represents the organized life and activities of all our local churches . . . *The Baptist* is a representative organ . . . and . . . must always preserve its representative capacity and be subject neither to official, personal or mass denomination." [3]

As for its editorial policies we read that

The Baptist is not the "private pulpit" of its editors. It is not for the propagation of their personal views. *The Baptist* does not claim to represent the theological opinions of individuals or of groups as such. It is not a fundamental organ. It is not a modernist organ. It is a Baptist organ . . . an organ for all genuine Baptist elements of the convention. . . . *The Baptist* cannot represent all of our Baptist people in their theological thinking. It can represent them in their practical work.[4]

The Baptist, if one may take the license to judge from the comments of other Baptist papers, may be said to represent the "liberal" element. "*The Baptist* . . . stands for the liberal party of our denomination. . . . "[5]

The Southern Convention has no such co-operative venture as *The Baptist.* In this grouping there are state or local papers. In the present study *The Word and Way,* a publication of the Missouri Baptists published in Kansas City, Missouri, was used. From accessible issues it seems evident that *The Word and Way* may be judged as representative of the opposition to what is the tenable position of *The Baptist,* since the latter notes with unique satisfaction "among the pleasures of life is finding ourselves in agreement with *The Word and Way.*" [6]

Both of the above periodicals were projected against a third magazine of the denomination, namely, *The Watchman-Examiner* which is called the "national paper of the Baptists." [7] It was hoped that a paper representative of the group as a whole would act as a balance between Northern and Southern sentiment. However, it is difficult to concede that the title is of real significance since its editors admit that as an organ of the Baptists it has not been representative of the denomination, although "we are doing our utmost to serve . . . every cause dear to the hearts of our Baptist people. It [*The Watchman-Examiner*] refuses to be the organ of any organization . . . because it reserves to itself the right to speak its own mind. . . ." [8]

It is an independently owned paper and in 1923 had a circulation of approximately 1,350,000. A contemporary publication

> like [s] the courage of *The Watchman-Examiner.* It comes out fearlessly in favor of the faith of the fathers. . . . It is not willing to blink at the fact that there are two tendencies among Baptists—conservatives and liberals. . . . It does not agree with *The Baptist,* which . . . said: "Let us now soft-pedal doctrinal differences." [9]

The Roman Catholic view on the manners and morals of the decade will be presented as it appeared in the *America* and *The Commonweal.* This latter publication was established in 1924, and it

> is a modern activity, suited to laymen who never speak authoritatively, but always tentatively. It can be carried on with a firm resolve to hate the Pharisee while taking the arm of the man in the street. We believe that such activity does not usurp work which others are trying to do, and that nobody else is at present so well prepared to do it as we our-

selves. . . . No other magazine frankly Catholic in character ever recruited so many good writers outside; and the quality of our pages is due in considerable measure to the fact that men and women of other beliefs have come here to talk things over, in a spirit of friendliness toward the age-old church which has a membership of the spirit as well as of the body.[10]

In announcing the appearance of the new Catholic weekly, *The Christian Register* felt that "nothing more interesting has been attempted in this country, and only in this country could such a thing be attempted. *The Commonweal* is a token of needed adaptation." [11]

The Commonweal occupies a unique position among the journals of the country. It most sincerely believes that the extension of the influence of the official Catholic press should be a prime duty incumbent upon every Catholic worthy of the name. . . . As *The Commonweal* conceives its own function, its part in the great work is to extend the influence of Catholicism into the secular world, particularly that part of the secular world interested in literature, art, and public affairs. . . .[12]

The Commonweal is committed to a belief that is the standard by which it selects and comments upon the events of the age. This belief is that many of the really chief events and circumstances of the times we live in—events and circumstances which are profoundly affecting the world—are not to be found among the startling and sensational things blazoned under huge headlines on front pages.[13]

The editors felt that ". . . the facts which prove the growing influence of *The Commonweal* are abundant and constantly increasing; . . . significant have been the widespread quotations from our pages by our . . . contemporaries, who recognize *The Commonweal* as the representative organ of the Catholic laity." [14] This is no idle boast, for allusions to the magazine are not only abundant but also very favorable. ". . . if the religious press in general was as courteous and as fairly conducted as is *The Commonweal* there would be little ground for criticism." [15] "We attach a very high value to *The Commonweal*. It presents Roman Catholicism at its best; and it is at its best that we wish to know it and to appreciate it." [16]

It is an "admirable journal, which is marvelously well edited by distinguished laymen of the communion." [17] "Discrimination, balance, and scholarly insight are habitual characteristics of *The Commonweal*, published by a group of Roman Catholic laymen as an organ of Catholic opinion." [18] "*The Commonweal* . . . a Roman

Catholic weekly [has] a fine spirit and breath of Christian sympathy [which] ought to commend it to a wide circle. . . ." [19] The organ of the United Lutherans alludes to it as "the Catholic weekly journal." [20]

The *America*, a weekly magazine published in New York under the editorship of Wilfred Parsons, S.J., has as its "chief aim to set forth without compromise or evasion Christian principles. As we wish to bring these principles into American life, so we also desire to imbue our non-Catholic and Catholic fellow citizens with the true spirit of Americanism." [21] It rates a recognition by contemporary publications about comparable to *The Commonweal*, although, in general, not so favorable.

It is recognized variously as "the organ of the Roman Catholic Church," [22] as a "Catholic Weekly," [23] "the Jesuit organ," [24] "the Jesuit weekly," [25] and "a weekly devoted to propaganda on behalf of the Roman cause." [26] While *The Christian Advocate* concedes that it "is one of our ablest and most interesting exchanges," [27] it does inject a caustic note. "The weekly journal which goes by the name of *America*, but which gets its keynote from Rome, reveals its non-American origin by the habitual tone in which it speaks of the founders of New England." [28] *America* receives almost constant attention from *The Lutheran*, as "an influential and widely read weekly," "a reliable Roman Catholic journal," "a credited organ of the Jesuit order." [29]

The official paper of the High Episcopalian Church is *The Living Church*, a weekly magazine published in Milwaukee. It "is definitely intended for the real thinkers, the educated minority, in the Church. Its discussions are intended not as instruction to the uninformed, but as contributions to the solution of the problems confronting the Church." [30] It is generally recognized as "official" by religious contemporary publications,[31] and looked upon as "our esteemed contemporary," [32] and as "one of the greater American religious weeklies. It represents the higher church group of Protestant Episcopalians, and . . . under the editorship of Dr. F. C. Morehouse, it had presented its views with vigor and ability." [33]

The American Hebrew is the principal magazine examined for expressions of public opinion among the Reform Jews. Known as the National Jewish Weekly, this periodical was established in 1879. Its founders, it would seem, were animated by a desire to make a vigorous struggle against religious radicalism and as a result involved themselves in controversies. These controversies culminated in the enumeration of a platform for Reform Judaism calling for

> . . . all that was true and noble in our religious life, the maintenance of the national existence as a constant factor, and the steadfast insistence upon the rights of the Jews. *The American Hebrew* stands for the promotion of a better understanding between Gentile and Jew in America. It aims at breaking down barriers that separate Gentile and Jew. It strives towards building bridges of good will that must unite Gentile and Jew for the sake of America.[34]

This magazine stands in a class apart when compared with the other religious periodicals examined. The general tone is definitely geared to a higher bracket of society, as is evidenced in its advertisements which cater to tastes for exotic perfumes, imported fashions, and the like. The pictures, too, have a different cast; for instance, one finds more examples of nudity, women smoking, and other illustrations of a similar vein. *The Commonweal* insists that "a general tone of alertness, generosity, and good will is admirable in itself, and . . . admirably characteristic as well of *The American Hebrew's* long and honorable tradition." [35] As an exchange of another Jewish publication, however, it is not received too kindly. "To consider seriously the reasoning of *The American Hebrew* would be folly. It is shameless and mendacious. . . ." [36] It "needs further instruction in American ideals and practices." [37]

The United Lutheran group opinion is represented in this study in *The Lutheran*. The United Lutheran Church was organized in 1918, and was an attempt at Lutheran unification. In 1922 it comprised about 3,800 congregations, and there were thirty-eight synods.[38] Its general policy is set forth by its editors,—"We try to inform our readers concerning what is going on within our boundaries." [39] By and large, the periodical is held in favor by other religious journals. "*The Lutheran* is a high-class denominational journal, the organ of the Lutheran Church in America. It is a stalwart defender of the Lutheran faith." [40] "The esteemed spokesman of the United Lutheran Church is an admirable publication." [41] It is not a magazine in the "liberal" camp, and this fact is noted by *The Christian Register*: ". . . it is little affected by the liberal, modernistic age." [42]

The *Lutheran Witness*, a biweekly published by Concordia Publishing House, Saint Louis, Missouri, is an official periodical of the Missouri Synod—a large group which remained outside the union in

1918. In 1923 the Synod extended from Maine to California and from Canada to the Gulf of Mexico with some 3,450 congregations, comprising twenty-seven Districts: twenty-three in the United States, three in Canada, and one in Brazil with a membership of 1,041,514.[43] A group of this size obviously required representation in this study. The editorial policy is clearly set forth:

> . . . the policy of this paper is to take up for discussion every salient issue arising in the Church. . . . It is the business of a church-organ to declare the teaching of that body which it serves, and which it is established to safeguard, so far as editors are able, against a perversion of its standards. This means that the various movements of the day which tend to break down Christianity must be exhibited in their true character.[44]

In 1784 American Methodism was organized. Sixty years later, in 1844, it was bisected because the Southern delegates believed that a provision of the constitution had been set aside by the Northern majority. Since that time the two wings have gone their own ways— the Northern group being known as the Methodist Episcopal Church; the Southern, as the Methodist Episcopal Church, South. A weekly periodical, *The Christian Advocate*, published in Nashville, Tennessee, is "the Southern Methodist official organ."[45] Rev. T. N. Ivey was elected editor by the General Conference in 1910 and was replaced by Alfred F. Smith in June, 1923. After this latter date, the paper assumed a somewhat different tone, and controversial issues, as well as comments on the manners and morals of the day, became less apparent. Throughout 1924 and 1925 the matter of unification was the issue of the day. By 1928 the paper had become more or less stereotyped. The paper was acclaimed as a "credit to the Church by its half sister in the North."[46]

". . . *The Christian Advocate*, New York, the official organ of the Methodist Church of this country,"[47] under the editorship of James R. Joy, entered "its hundredth year [1925] with the established reputation of being the most widely circulated Methodist weekly in the world"[48] with a weekly circulation of 51,012.[49] It is "the most successful denominational paper in America. . . . No other denominational paper compares with it in circulation. . . ."[50] "This paper grows stronger and better every day. Methodism may well be proud of it."[51]

Two magazines, one representative of the "conservative" and the other of the "liberal" groups within the Presbyterian denomination are *The Presbyterian Magazine* and *The Presbyterian Banner*. The former, a monthly publication, "an organ of the conservative, perhaps the militantly orthodox section of the Presbyterian Church, U. S. A." [52] is entitled the "official medium of the Presbyterian Church, U. S. A." [53] The present magazine is an outcome of more than a century of publication and experiment "and is probably the oldest religious periodical in the world that can show a continuous publication." [54] Its present name was substituted for the *New Era Magazine* in 1921. *The Presbyterian Magazine* is

> . . . the organ of the entire church, . . . the servant of the church and comes not to be ministered unto but to minister. It . . . endeavors to be an informative and educational, unifying and energizing agency in the work of the church, binding together all its branches of activity into co-operative harmony and efficiency and inspiring them with a common spirit of service. . . . Controversy and partisanship will not mar or mark its pages, and it will seek to be a bond and medium of unity and fellowship and helpfulness and good cheer. [55]

Various Boards, such as Temperance, Moral, Education, and Ministerial Relief are accorded space in different issues. Hence, editorials, as such, do not treat manners and morals except in a cursory way, due, obviously, to the space allocations to separate agencies.

The Presbyterian Banner, a weekly magazine published in Pittsburgh, "belongs to a progressive minority, sometimes called modernist." [56] On the occasion of its 115th anniversary, a Baptist contemporary proffered congratulations to its editor, Dr. James H. Snowden. "He and his helpers are making an admirable paper." [57]

And now we come to our final periodical. *The Christian Register*, a weekly publication under the editorship of Dr. Albert C. Dieffenbach, ". . . makes a plea for the simple, liberal, informal religion of the followers of Jesus, for the spirit of toleration, for dissent against the episcopacy of the English, and for the spirit of free inquiry of the early New England settlers." [58] The editor

> . . . never assumes that he speaks *ex cathedra*. He speaks what he himself believes. That is why his name stands in the masthead at the top of the editorial page. He is personally responsible for every line in the paper. His authority in opinion is nothing. Unitarianism is in no respect a religion of authority. [59]

Contemporary periodicals of various denominations are one in their accord that it is "the official organ of the Unitarians." [60]

It will be helpful when reading the editorial comments later on in this study to recall the position of these periodicals as outlined in this chapter. In most instances the view will be conditioned by the prospectus.

And now, before proceeding immediately to the press utterances, it is meet that we turn our attention briefly to the pattern of life in the Twenties against which editors of the religious press raised their voices. The following chapter will attempt to give a general but hasty glance at the politico-economic phase of the picture. A succeeding chapter will begin the discussion of the socio-cultural aspects. This will be done in considerable detail since these facets of life in the 1920's are the burden of the present work.

"Such men
I never saw, nor shall I see again."

—Nestor.

CHAPTER III

The Dismal Decade

There has never been an age when a warning of the backward trend has not been sounded by someone belonging to it. Perhaps the minds of men, like their eyes, change as they grow older, and they see better the things that are far away than those that are near. The past gathers a halo around it. If ever there were ominous shaking of heads over "this generation," the halcyon days of the 1920's received it.

In this chapter we will look briefly at this era "so sorely out of joint" that it called forth the alarming attention of the religious press to sound the tocsin of a vanishing culture. Mark Sullivan notes that the manners and morals of America's young people especially were a source of worried interest on the part of editors.[1]

To the younger generation of the decade, the era appears to have been accepted as truly the "golden age." Indeed, by contrast with the Thirties, it was a time when money came easily and doubts and fears about the future did not exist. Although in the effulgence of the glittering glow there was a smooth and ready acceptance of the prevailing order by the younger set, there was an unwearied speculation on the part of those not so young—a speculation culminating in no settled conclusions over "the era of wonderful nonsense" and "the absorption in tremendous trifles." By and large, the vantage point provided by the passage of thirty years enables one today to conclude that the tone of American society was in many ways very unhealthy. The story of this gay, irresponsible era of disillusionment could be told in many ways, for in the froth and turmoil of these years tremendous changes took place in American society. However, in accord with the purpose of this study, as stated earlier, primary emphasis will be placed upon the social and cultural aspect of life, and the public reaction, as evidenced in the religious periodical press, to the pattern of the manners and morals.

In 1920 Warren G. Harding became President of the United States. It is probably true that his election was due, in no small part, to his campaign promise to bring the country back to normalcy. War-weary and disillusioned by promises and attempts at making and preserving peace abroad—promises and attempts which never materialized—the people in 1920 were anxious and willing to devote primary attention generally to life in these United States and particularly as the living of that life pertained to themselves and to their personal interests. If the world had not been made safe for democracy by war, at least the United States would be made a paradise for its citizens by normalcy. In retrospect, it becomes obvious that this panacea of normalcy had unique ingredients. Perhaps the main constituent from which all others drew their source is one which might be termed conservative politics colored by a narrow nationalism. The business of government was not the government of business. Definitely "the business of America is business," and business included speculation in stocks and real estate, high-pressure salesmanship and installment buying, and advertising. As ideals lost their meaning in the wake of World War I, financial success became for the average American the one goal of life, and activities which involved the making of money assumed an importance unparalleled in previous eras.

Speculation was not something new or a phenomenon peculiar to the Twenties, but it had never been pursued so vigorously by so many people—a fact well verified by the nationwide repercussions felt from a shock on Wall Street in October, 1929. The salesman and the advertising man, freed from many scruples that curtailed questionable methods of an earlier age, adroitly convinced Americans that former luxuries were present necessities, and thus a whetted appetite for more and better comforts and conveniences led to unparalleled installment buying.

The tremendous industrial expansion accelerated in great part by the automobile, moving picture, and radio industries was regarded as a presage of limitless prosperity. In the dizzying whirl of economic advance, a nation enjoying the highest standard of living it had ever attained was not likely to ponder too deeply or too seriously over any change in social values consequent upon the economic advance.

Good times had not followed immediately after the war. Readjustment necessary to gear the economic pattern to peace-time living brought a recession in 1921 which produced a momentary industrial stagnation. The collapse of expanding agricultural markets injured the farmer more critically than the business man or average wage-earner. By 1922, however, the United States had made a round-about face and industry surged ahead with eager hope. Domestic markets revived and pent-up consumer demands easily handled production. The expanding domestic market, supplemented by a growing foreign trade, gave industry an added incentive. People were producing more, earning more, and spending more than ever before. President Hoover in 1928 could proudly boast that "We in America are nearer to the final triumph over poverty than ever before. . . . We have not yet reached the goal, but given a chance to go forward . . . we shall soon, with the help of God, be in sight of the day when poverty shall be banished from this nation." It might be noted in passing that the huge national income which naturally rose in response to advances in industry and manufacturing was by no means evenly distributed among American families—but relative gains on all levels helped to lull the citizens into a state of false security.

As business became more consolidated it drew the reins tighter with the result that labor unions lost many of the gains made during the war years. But since wages were generally higher than 1914 levels, and welfare capitalism in various areas seemed to better the workers' lot without organization, labor made no serious efforts to reassert its former position or to penetrate new industries.

Agriculture's relative share in national income lagged behind that of industry and of labor. The farmer had never recovered from the postwar recession and the prosperity he had known in wartime remained but a cherished memory.

The amazing progress in the economic sphere eclipsed everything else in the history of the Nineteen-twenties. Immediate gains tended to obscure basic defects. Truly, nothing succeeds like success. Government placed its benediction upon the new rugged individualism, and laws, boards, and agencies enacted or erected to curb business were practically suspended or converted into advisory commissions in the interests of *laissez-faire.* The people were quite willing to uphold the governmental attitude in letting industry have its way and asked nothing more than to be left free to make money and to spend money.

The nationalistic spirit of the age is well summed up in the popular slogan "One Hundred Per Cent Americanism." The hostility toward all things alien assumed new forms of organized intolerance, such as the Ku Klux Klan. This movement originating in 1915 had no connection with the Klan of the post-Civil War period. It wielded quite a political influence in the Twenties but by the end of the decade had spent itself and lost most of its momentum.

The immigration legislation of the period is indicative, also, of narrow nationalism which brought about a complete reversal of our traditional policy in regard to the immigrant. The fear of Communism had been effectively played up to exert pressure for the curtailment of immigration and the conservative elements in American life remained vigilant in repressing all radical influences and led to the so-called Red baiting of the 1920's.

This brief resumé should suffice. With the political scene little more than a pale reflection of the economic pattern and governmental leadership being more often in Wall Street than in Washington, repercussions will not be found wanting on other levels of American life.

In an age that was caught up in the flood tide of material satisfactions, it was to be expected that a revolt against the restraints placed on conduct would become evident one way or the other. It is difficult—if not impossible—to decide on definite variations in the amount of immorality in any given period or periods. But it is obvious in looking back that the postwar reaction from idealism notable in all areas was especially so in the sphere of manners and morals. It is to this aspect of American social and cultural living that we now turn. That there were indubitable symptoms of a weakening of the moral fiber no one can deny.

"Where an opinion is general,
it is usually correct."

—Jane Austen, *Mansfield Park.*
Chapter XI.

CHAPTER IV

The Sins of Society

From the vantage point provided by the passage of time, the decade of the 1920's, in spite of its material prosperity, appears to have been a period of moral disintegration and intellectual confusion. And those who would attempt to explain or characterize the era solely in politico-economic terms are probably missing important factors that gave the decade its own peculiar notes. It is apparent that beneath the advancing prosperity and the rising standard of living, a confusion of ideas, an uprooting of former mores, and a revolution in the mode of living were taking place.

It is usually conceded that the era spells out a reaction to the tense idealism that characterized the first seventeen years of the century in its crusading for broader social justice. By 1919, in the aftermath of war that had been fought apparently to no purpose, a wave of cynicism replaced the previous idealism. Youth, in particular, seemed eager to relax, to enjoy itself, to question the traditional moral and religious bases of society traced out by its elders—bases which now to the younger set seemed to be shot through with greed, hypocrisy, and suspicion.

However, since it is not the purpose of this study to probe for reasons as to the decadence of the era, it accepts the fact of a moral degeneracy and proceeds to inquire to what degree religious leaders of the day were aware of the contemporary revolt.

Ever since man's first revolt, it has been necessary to reckon with the future. The ancients examined the entrails of sacrificial animals or listened to the incantations of infuriated priestesses for guidance. Gazing into the depths of a crystal ball is still in vogue. However eager man has been to probe the future, seldom has he appraised his own day with any marked degree of objectivity. It is precisely on this score that the editors of our religious periodicals step up to claim the palm. From their editorials it is obvious that they were keenly alerted to the revolt that was taking place in the realm of manners and morals. *The American Hebrew*, although liberal in its general attitude, was not inclined to write off events of its own day as inconsequential. "Unquestionably today there is a scrapping of conventions and an inauguration of freedom which are confounding to the do-as-you're-told school of adults. Boys and girls with astonishing frankness are doing as they like and very often what they like is good neither for them nor for us." [1]

Too, the editors of the Lutheran organs examined in this study agree that the days are critical—"a time when parents in the home and preachers in the pulpit need to burn with holy wrath against the evils of the day." [2] "Pleasure-Wild and Enjoyment-Crazy" are terms used to describe the people of the time. "The words carry a stern indictment . . . but they are absolutely true to fact. The carousals, debauchery, wild dances, low shows, reckless pleasure rides, and other frivolous indecencies,—all tell the same story." [3]

The journals regard the effects of the "high-pressure living, such as has become an obsession with Americans generally" [4] as anything but wholesome. "It has made us the most extravagant, the most reckless, and the most nerve-wracked people in the world," [5] and this "extravagance is sinful, wicked, and ruinous." [6] The editorials in both periodicals are intent to alert their readers to some very basic facts about the crisis the age is facing. "Unbridled license is in the swing at present, as has never been the case in our history. Pleasures are taking a vulgar and sensuous turn. . . . Modesty and innocence . . . are fast vanishing. . . . Nearly anything becomes proper now." [7] "Moral conditions were never worse in America than they are today. Crime wave upon crime wave of embezzlement, forgery, burglary, murder, and arson have swept over our country. Our city streets have never been so unsafe, and human life has never been so uncertain." [8] "We are not only wasting our material resources at an alarming rate, but our physical, moral, and religious energies as well." [9]

Warnings abound as to what the future of civilization and culture will be.

We will soon be a nation without ideals—without morality and religion. The words which are applied to the prodigal who "wasted his substance" express what is wrong with us as a nation. . . . It is amazing how near the level of crass materialism and epicureanism even church members and Christians seem ready to descend. . . . We are fast drifting into paganism.[10]

Indeed, the days are evil, but still there is not a trace of despair in the comments. Religion must have a place—its rightful place in the lives of people. Readers are exhorted to render to God His due.

Paul tells us that in the last days—and those are our days—men shall be "lovers of pleasure more than lovers of God." God condemns this pleasure-wild and enjoyment-crazy love of the world. Not that He would rob us of joy and gladness, mirth and happiness. . . . Let it be said as emphatically as anything can be said that God is the only Author of genuine and lasting pleasure. All things that give us happiness are His gifts.[11]

"The real root of evil is irreligion." [12]

The picture that both periodicals paint is sketched in somber tones. However, it might be noted that the blame for the sorry state of society is not placed at the feet of youth alone. In fact, there are evidences that the editors would admonish those who tend to do so. "One must remember that the youth of today and the youth of a generation or two ago are just as different as the times are different." [13]

We find in these same years that public opinion, as expressed in the Unitarian journal, is inclined to be very indulgent in its appraisal of the period. While it does not scruple to assert that the decade beginning with 1925 may pass into history as an unconventional age when a ruthless invasion of conventions, sacred and time-honored, has been made, it hazards the opinion that this age, in the main, is a wholesome one.[14]

Viewing life in all its aspects, what it was, what it is, we incline toward the opinion that there is enough sense, health of body and soul, ease and genuineness to keep us hopeful. . . . We may have lost in some particulars, but we have gained enough, more in others, to more than compensate for the loss. To an outlook not warped by jealousies nor embittered by disappointments and reverses, the decade which we are entering is the best of all, unconventional though it is.[15]

Further, the so-called "revolt of youth" is half-myth and youth is too much talked about. But there are always among us persons who simply must start something. Otherwise they perish. If to their creative gift they add the gift of speech and of writing, their propulsive powers are increased an hundredfold. . . . This is the day of conventions, of resolutions, protests, campaigns, and urgent books made overnight. So it has befallen youth. Youth in metamorphosis! Nothing is more exaggerated than the impression that youth is now profoundly different from the youth of yesterday. Those who were youths then simply grew up without the aid of propaganda.[16]

Too long and too loud have journalists, preachers, and all who have the ear of the public been dinning audiences with the statement that this is a degenerate age, basing their arguments on "the daily spectacle of extravagance, clamor, 'jazzy music,' indecent entertainment, and frivolity" [17] which have made young people incapable of serious thought. It is conceded, nonetheless, that the era is a "gilded age; those who have money are spending it; those who lack money are resorting to various devices, legal and illegal, to get it." [18] Indeed, the age is one to turn the head of youth, but, like its Lutheran neighbors, Unitarian opinion believes that "we must not charge the young with the full responsibility. Boys and girls are only aping their elders." [19]

In 1926, looking back over the past few years, the journal assumes an attitude that an admirable balance has been established and the day of hearing about " 'youth in revolt,' 'flaming youth,' 'young people who flouted parental authority,' petted, danced, smoked, and cut the lines of traditional restraint" [20] is passed. Parents have despaired, guardians of public morals have expressed indignation, reformers have had their day and say. "Most young men and women today—as well as yesterday and the same will be true tomorrow—are idealists, obey the law both moral and civil, and aim higher than the thrill of the passing hour." [21] "We are witnessing the glad free life which can take far better care of itself than the elder generation did in its juvenile time, even though certain outward things appear a bit askew." [22]

A segment of Catholic opinion, as expressed in *The Commonweal*, feels in common with the above group that conditions have undergone a radical change. Its attitude is at once aware of the passing of the comfortable old way of life and at the same time somewhat querulous with those who see nothing but menacing clouds before them. In an evidently intentional satirical vein it calls to task some of the reformers who have all the answers. It would give the palm of victory for a revelation—both definite and succinct—to a certain recognized authority on diet and cooking that morality depends on the right use being made of the right foods. *The Commonweal* sees many new fields for investigation and speculation thrown open to eager students of research. It gives a few topical suggestions.

> What relationship can be established between the country church supper and the rise of the Ku Klux Klan? What evidence exists that Judge Ben Lindsey supped every night on Welsh rarebit, fried oysters, and mince pie while preparing *The Revolt of Modern Youth?* What dishes are served at the luncheon of a certain board dedicated to moral reform?[23]

In the same tenor it notes with some marked satisfaction that "the youth in America seems to have outgrown the period when it was desperately written about and analyzed. People are beginning to take it for granted that neither bobbed hair nor the saxophone was the ultimate distinguishing characteristic of perverse Babylonian architecture." [24]

For that fraction of Catholic thought which the *America* represents, the decade is neither a cloudless horizon nor a reserve of moral rectitude. "Laxity persists . . . [and] . . . is getting more widespread and more marked, and the eyes of thinking men are being opened to the fact that we have got into a spiritual mess that demands immediate remedial measures." [25] This journal seems to speak for a more serious group and in piquant tones is not slow to decry many modern thinkers who "try to batter down all rules governing human conduct and social decency . . . [who] shout their views in radical journals that are so advanced that they cannot keep pace even with themselves." [26] Censured are those who would sanction the new mores and advocate "the so-called new morals of the twentieth century for the age-old morals that have well served all the Christian centuries of the past." [27] In reality, the new morals are only the older morals of a pagan day—"a renaissance of the system that the morals of Christianity supplanted." [28] The journal cannot impress its audience too weightily that

> . . . there is nothing faulty in these so-called old morals; they are neither antiquated nor misfits. They are new with each new generation and they are still capable of raising to a high and noble standard all

who practice them. They can redeem society if they are given a fair chance. They make for peace and happiness and love; they establish a home and sanctify marriage; they stabilize society and they prepare the way for future happiness after death. But the new morals create a social state that is divorced from reason and ruled by irrational passion, a society that must result in a collection of feverish, restless, broken-hearted derelicts. When the appetites are dominant, there can be no happiness or true love. The new morals deify the body and pander to the passions; the old morals keep one close to God.[29]

A rather strong indictment is leveled against youth at the mid-decade, and public opinion, in the columns of *America,* is not willing to exonerate youth, as some other groups are inclined to do. It complains that "the younger generation is demanding freedom, but from what it wishes to be free is not wholly clear." [30] In fact, freedom as envisioned by youth is merely a type of bondage.

A "flapper" can think herself independent even when she depends daily on a row of pots of paints and pomades. Her flag of freedom is a pair of lips that imitate a gash hastily inflicted by an unskilled surgeon. Her liberty hall is a beauty parlor where she sits in bondage to a parcel of barbers who put mud on her face and pull out her eyebrows.[31]

A divergence as great as that here evidenced in Catholic opinion is likewise discernible in Presbyterian sentiment. The "conservative" *Presbyterian Magazine,* in an attempt to give a literally true and vividly realistic diagnosis of the sin-sick world, turns back the pages of history to let the ancient prophet thunder forth:

Oh, sinful nation, a people laden with iniquity, a seed of evil-doers, children that deal corruptly! The whole head is sick, and the whole heart is faint. From the sole of the foot even unto the head there is no soundness in it; but wounds, and bruises, and fresh stripes; they have not been closed, neither bound up, neither mollified with oil.[32]

With the same literary fluency the journal further expresses its grim opinion that the present generation is perilously close to danger and disaster—that the "crust of civilization" is thin under its feet.

The Great War swept the ocean of the world with the fiercest storm of history, and it takes a long time for such a commotion, that sends its waves dashing up against every shore and rolling into every bay and far up every inlet, to subside into its normal calm. The world has been convulsed . . . and every field of thought and action has been disturbed. . . . The forces of reaction against conservatism have been unloosed and have threatened to overturn the very foundations of peace and order. The most settled principles and laws of society . . . have been attacked.[33]

Straight thinking—there is a tremendous amount of the other kind of thinking that is going on—is necessary if Americans are to get out of the present turmoil. "The world's sense of proportions is badly out of joint. Its power to appraise values is . . . not functioning in a . . . normal manner." [34]

Some attempt is made to index partially, as it were, the evils of the age. "The novel and theater and moving picture, the dance and jazz music, excitement and noises are more and more absorbing our time and energies. Increasing numbers are always craving for a crowd and itching for a new thrill. . . ." [35] Moving into the very practical realm, opinion recounts figures to bolster its position.

Eleven million American people visit the moving picture show every day. . . . The bill for cosmetics alone now calls for over seven hundred million dollars a year. . . . Ice cream and candy cost us more than our religion. . . . The tobacco bill is something mountainous, and one trust alone spends eleven million dollars a year in advertising its products.[36]

Woe to the generation that does not realize that "sin is the cancerous root of all the sores of our world." [37]

Even a small sampling of expressions of opinion, as presented in *The Presbyterian Banner*, is indicative that the editors are in the school of thought at variance with their Presbyterian contemporaries immediately consulted above. American youth "are receiving considerable blame for being undisciplined, emotional, erratic, and defiant towards law and authority." [38] But fundamentally youth has not changed, except for the better. Some conventions may be discarded but youth "still clings to the best in the old civilization and is creating better standards in the new." [39] The periodical evinces the belief that it is a fatal mistake to magnify pessimistically certain tendencies of modern life. "Many things," it adds, "that were possible and lovely in the past have gone beyond recall and new conditions must be met." [40]

And still editorial pens continue to dip deep into the stream of life in its complexities!

The organ of Episcopalian thought alludes, in but isolated instances, to the manners and morals of the day—but in its terseness, the position of the group it represents is unequivocal. Youth today is unfortunately setting the pace. In a reminiscent tone it recalls the day when youth copied age—when to appear a man was the height of youthful ambition, but all this belongs to another age. Now age copies youth.

> Grandma bobs her hair and puts rouge on her face. Grandpa puts away the pipe of dignity for the cigaret of impudence; and even the clergy, once a bulwark of conservatism, are found seriously considering youth's views on religion and advocating serving up religion and morals in a form sufficiently palatable to tempt the jaded appetite of blasé youth.[41]

With nostalgic note, it rues this day when "age has lost its nerve." [42]

Group opinion of the Methodists and Baptists still remains for consideration. In the former denomination, the Southern journal is more articulate than its Northern counterpart. The Nashville publication, speaking for its section, indicates that opinion is alerted to what it terms "the new rebellion—a retrogression back to the days of Rome's decadence [when] the masses had but one cry: 'Bread and the Circus.' " [43] There is cause for faintheartedness as it admits that "with multitudes life is nothing but a giggle. They cannot think, they cannot read." [44] In the olden days "a favorite theme of preachers and orators was 'The hand that rocks the cradle rules the world.' Of course, this is all wrong since times have changed and people are becoming civilized. It is now heathenish to have a cradle to rock." [45]

With many of their contemporaries, the Methodists concur that the rebellion of adults is a greater danger to civilization than the so-called revolt of youth.

> Mature persons hitherto have been supposed to have had opportunities for knowing the value of tested and approved authority and therefore to have come to possess reverence for it. . . . But now from the circle of the older men and women come objections which proclaim a new independence, a freedom from the bondage of all moral considerations.[46]

This strange twist in modern society—adult anarchists—is one of the most alarming conditions of the day.

In its own name, the journal expressing opinion of Methodists in the Northern group is not too vocal but it begs permission to "shout an old-fashioned Methodist 'Amen' " [47] to the plaints of contemporaries that boys and girls are being lost in "Folly Lane." Heedful of ⌐ ⌐litions, too, are the Baptist journals. *The Baptist* notes with some disquietude that

> eating, playing, and dressing are the serious business of life to multitudes, while praying and giving and working are side issues, if indeed they have any place at all. Butterfly life is in the ascendance and everywhere conspicuous. But butterfly life, if brilliant, is short and the ending dark. And the generation of butterflies is living a life which leads nowhere.[48]

There is no doubt but that a mental and moral cyclone is sweeping across the land,[49] and if this is the way back to normalcy—losing our high ideals and our splendid goals—this group is willing to lose the flag.[50]

In answer to the self-posed question as to whether the world is growing better or worse, *The Word and Way* optimistically replies that the generation appears to be covetous, avaricious, greedy and unsurpassed by any preceding generation; that Christianity is in a "topsy-turvy" situation; that worldliness is in the church and a rank materialistic philosophy in the schools. Notwithstanding, several conditions give renewed hope to this group of Baptists "that the Kingdom is coming and that the heathen will be given to our Lord for his inheritance and the uttermost part of the earth for his possession." [51] One such condition is the widespread investigation of religious issues, and another is the spirit of liberality to be found in the present generation. The lawlessness of the day is thus more apparent than usual.[52]

It remains for our final periodical to give voice to the sentiment of the remaining segment of groups being considered. Its diagnosis is detailed, its prognosis, disheartening.

> The world is sick and it is not suffering from a skin disease. It has faint heart action, high blood pressure; it has lost its balance-sense of rhythm. It has lived on sweets and highly seasoned foods so long that it has intestinal indigestion. Its moral muscles are flabby, and it walks haltingly along the old paths. It does not dare to make the new paths over the mountains. Its sense of touch is weakened. Its hands are red with blood. It sees through a glass darkly. It hears indistinctly the

voices of its prophets. It smells no longer the odor of foam from the infinite sea of truth. Its instincts seem dulled. Its sense of direction is weak, its ideas of proportion are faulty, its moral perspective is distorted. It is trembling from shellshock, censorious, querulous, selfish, revengeful, immoral, epileptic, hysterical. It has the suicidal mania. It is sick and sad and heavy with sorrows.[53]

All has been said! The comments here run the gamut of sentiments ranging from the droll to the dismal, from the sanguine to the futile. But an unmistakable constant is woven throughout the expressions of opinion, namely, that the decade is an erratic one. It is, of course, granted that variables are discernible. Public opinion will be seen to have differed in its approval or disapproval of apparent and radical changes, in its commendation or condemnation of youth, in its presage for weal or for woe of the future, in its hope or in its despair.

A salient fact to be noted at this point is that opinion in the Twenties was in no mood to remain silent. In the following chapters, we shall attempt to spotlight certain features characteristic of the age, and then to listen as public sentiment speaks its mind.

"On all sides, from innumerable tongues
A dismal hiss, the sound
Of public scorn."

—Milton, *Paradise Lost.*

CHAPTER V

Speed—Sports—The Spectacular

Were it possible to turn back the clock of time and to find one-self in the midst of the milieu that made up life in the 1920's, it is probably true that one of the obvious features uniquely characteristic of the age would be its restlessness—a hankering to veer away from the staid and platitudinous existence of the "Victorian Age"—a restlessness gestated from the confused weaving of the new and old in American life. A highly potent contributing factor to this unrest was certainly that device which gave wheels to the nation and put it in motion as it had never been before, namely, the automobile.

In the postwar years the automobile industry became a token of American prosperity and it is true beyond question that the industry was the key industry in those days—not only prosperous itself but contributing largely to the prosperity of the country.[1] Originating near the end of the nineteenth century, it developed into spectacular proportions in the Twenties. Before the war, motor cars were largely restricted to the wealthy and middle class.

> Half a block, half a block,
> Half a block onward,
> All in their automobiles
> Rode the Four Hundred.[2]

By 1920, however, the ownership of an automobile was no longer a class distinction. Small cars, such as the famous Model T Fords, were manufactured at prices low enough to make cars available to the general public.[3]

As it came, the automobile changed the face of America and con-ditioned life in its every aspect. The economic, political, and social implications of the expansion of the automotive industry would be difficult to overestimate,[4] and an examination of any one of these aspects might well prove an inexhaustive study. However, our attention is to be focused on the automobile as society saw it in its social ramifications.[5]

To one anxious to sound the pulse of contemporary public opinion on the place of the automobile in society of the 1920's it seems that the Baptist denomination, if one judge from editorial comment, is most keenly alerted to the over-all picture. This group views democracy being worked out in the realm of the practical in the fact that "more than 200,000 automobiles are rushing hither and thither . . . driven by ordinary folks." [6] Assuredly, the automobile holds a secure place in our modern life and "its practical uses are so many and so well known that it is unnecessary to list them," [7] but inevitably "such an agent will be used for illegitimate as well as legitimate purposes." [8] And it is over the former that public opinion feels it a duty to speak.

For crime, the automobile is an invaluable ally. "Thieves and murderers have discovered that the automobile is an instrument made to their hands and are using it increasingly." [9] It is not, however, in crimes against property that the use of the automobile is most to be feared. "Morals are more important than money, and the corruption of the young means more to any community than the looting of many banks." [10] Baptist sentiment feels that the time has come for a frank recognition of this great evil which has grown up in connection with the automobile. Bypassing it is no longer feasible in the light of figures showing that "automobile rides furnished the occasion for ninety-five per cent of the moral lapses in two hundred cases of delinquency among girls." [11]

> Because it is not considered just nice to talk about such things, we have ignored horrible conditions or contented ourselves with whispering about them. . . . Only action on the part of the public will reduce this evil to a minimum. . . . The state can better afford to increase its police force than by inertness to allow this carnival of lust to go unchecked.[12]

Lamentably true is it that "we have lapsed into a state of indifference, or at least of inactivity, regarding that which is of primary importance to our civilization. . . . It is time to wake up." [13]

Opinion likewise notes that there are some other undesirable ways in which the increasing popularity of the automobile manifests itself other than in unchaperoned use by boys and girls. "Pastors have been complaining that their church members are prone to forsake the Sunday service for jaunts to the country." [14] With fervid religious emotion the group considers the possibility or feasibility of "Christian men who use motor cars to reach their church services [carrying] some kind of refined but univerally used placard or pennant which would signify that the car was being used with a religious end in view," [15] and decides that since "Christian people dislike to mingle on the highway with the great host of Sunday desecrators" [16] the idea might be practically considered.

The speed of the automobile is deplored, and the denomination with a nostalgic tone recalls that

> In the "dear dead days of long ago," somewhere far back in almost prehistoric times, horses drew buggies, and surreys, and carrioles, and victorias—how weirdly those archaic names strike upon our ears—along our city streets. Things then went very well. The age of speed had not come. . . . Now our western civilization is on . . . wheels, riding at breakneck speed. . . . In our restless, inconsequent, and rapid living age have we time for the things worth while?[17]

The alarming number of fatalities is proof secure that "safety from fast-flying cars . . . [is] impossible," [18] and the sorry fact is "we are really getting to the point where we are afraid to walk the streets." [19]

With the ever-increasing number of cars, and with the ever-increasing recklessness in driving, the problem of safety is further entangled by intoxication, for although a "great majority of accidents . . . is due to reckless driving . . . in not a few cases the drivers were drunk." [20]

> Drunken motorists are everywhere running down men, women, and children. . . . It is getting dangerous for the most careful driver to take his machine out of his garage.[21]

This religious group would tender congratulations to those judges who treat the drunken motorist as they would a homicidal maniac.

Inexperienced and irresponsible drivers are also called to task.

> Any day one may see a powerful machine driven by a boy in his teens who sits on his backbone and rushes his car along a crowded street. Young girls are allowed to drive cars which should be trusted only to mature and experienced drivers.[22]

Inaction and indecision are corroding society. "A few cases of a plague . . . sets the whole country buzzing; hundreds are killed by carelessness and we dismiss the matter with a mild 'too bad.' How long, O Lord, how long?" [23]

Taking a rapid glance back on Baptist opinion, it is seen that the denomination was not only articulate but that the members of the Baptist communion stood shoulder to shoulder with no dissenting voices to mar the harmony of agreement.

Sparing in printers' ink and succinct in editorial comment, *The American Hebrew* and the Jewish population it represents remark in passing that "the automobile, useful servant of man, is at times his Nemesis." [24]

The Episcopalian segment of the population considers that automobile legislation—flagrant in its violation—is a moral responsibility, and the group evinces deep concern "about our profession of Christ's religion and the disregard of the sacredness of our lives and that of others in the nonobservance of letter and spirit of automobile legislation." [25] Writing in midsummer with the tourist season in flower, a note of urgency underlies the anxiety over the condition of the conscience of the Churchman, who, after attending 'Golf Mass' on Sunday morning

> "steps on her" to see how quickly he can convey himself and family to pleasant outdoor recreation spots; of the consistency of the parson who, after beseeching the good Lord to hear us for those who travel by land, drives his lowly Lizzie or his lordly Lincoln chainless or with worn brake-bands, and makes his boast that she or it can pass anything on the road. [26]

The frightful toll of human lives exacted in accidents should, it is hoped, arouse the nation's conscience.

Turning the spotlight on Catholic opinion, we find it commenting upon the age which it sees remarkable for its achievements but just as remarkable for its reversals of the past. "Not more than a few years ago, automobiles were for the exclusive use of the rich. . . . This has changed. . . . Even the poorest person is begged by installment men to accept Ford machines." [27] Unfortunately, safety and the automobile are still contrasted in American experience, and sobering, indeed, is the increasing number of lives snuffed out in motor accidents daily. [28] The *America* is in accord with its contemporary. According to statistics that found their way into the hands of the editor, the journal sees that one of the chief causes of deaths in the United States is the automobile. "It appears to have a habit of falling over embankments, stalling in front of the limited express, and running down timid pedestrians, that is almost incurable." [29]

Since advertising has little effect upon those who need proof that carefulness is a virtue,[30] legislation to reduce the danger to a minimum is to be sought. Let no one doubt but that "it will be perfectly possible to secure proper legislation regarding the use of the automobile and to enforce it." [31] Eternal vigilance must be expended if we are to advance beyond the habit of offering annual holocausts to speed.

Sweeping statements are always dangerous and seldom correct. Especially applicable, the *America* reasons, is this maxim to those who would place all blame for social disorders on the automobile. "If we wish to attack the problem of adult or juvenile delinquency squarely, we must examine intrinsic causes." [32] More correctly we are justified, opinion asserts, "in attributing the growing moral maladjustment to a neglect of those influences which would dispose the youthful mind to use the creature within its compass with sane and balanced judgment." [33] The automobile is definitely a force to be reckoned with in society, but Catholic sentiment is anxious that cure be applied to the root. Unless education supplies the influences needed for full living, history will repeat itself, and the dissolution of modern society will follow as inevitably as did that of Greece and Rome.

The Lutheran attitude is one of anxious distress over the speed mania that has become epidemic, and it repines over a fond memory when "men used to travel at the rate of ten or fifteen miles an hour with a spirited horse to set the pace." [34] Unfortunately, people today crave thrills. "Like children on a toboggan railway they delight in moving through life at a rate of speed that takes the breath and makes the hair stand on end." [35] With speed an obsession in all departments of human activity

> need we wonder that life has become a restless turmoil, a fitful chase after things that do not satisfy man's deepest wants? Need we wonder that nerves are being racked and that the most prevalent and stubborn diseases that physicians have to deal with are nervous diseases?[36]

The second Lutheran periodical gives a reassuring nod to what its contemporary denominational journal has uttered. It, too, feels that the speed problem of the automobile has not been solved despite "licenses, traffic laws, traffic police, one-way streets, parking regulations, speed limits, chauffeur examinations, signals, warnings, auto clubs, and a few more things." [37] But it wonders if perchance a solution has not been bypassed. It would like to propose an answer: Godliness, and then goes on to expatiate:

> The old saying which tells us what happens when wealth accumulates and men decay is still true. And no nation, no people, not even the American nation, can alter that. . . . There is absolutely no substitute for genuine godliness. . . . We do not say "the cursed automobile," for the automobile is not to blame for its abuse. But we say: "O the cursed religious indifference which admires the works of man and pays no attention to the wonderful and only saving work of God in the hearts of man." [38]

Both Methodist organs indicate that group opinion in this section regards the progress that has been made in the production and use of the automobile in a quarter of a century as truly stupendous. "We do not see how we could get along without the 'auto' " [39] but the devil's use of it levels a serious indictment against it:

> It is being used as an engine of destruction making robbery and murder simple and unrequited, causing the loss of thousands of lives by accidents and the crippling of countless children; pimp of flashy roadhouses. . . . The automobile is clearly unregenerate. With all the safeguards of the law thrown about it, it continues to be the greatest fomenter of injury, manslaughter, murder, unhappiness, and crime in general. [40]

In addition to this scathing diatribe, the group has comments to contribute relative to the speed aspect of the automobile—and it is just as distressing to the Methodist section as it is to their contemporaries. "American people are going nowhere at the rate of sixty miles an hour," [41] and it is this

> mania for speed which at least partly explains the significant figures on losses of life due to accidents on American highways. . . . Our casualties occur at the rate of one every forty-two seconds, the rate steadily increasing with each year. [42]

Indeed, "the pedestrian in any large city takes his life in his hands when he leaves his home," [43] and it is to be borne in mind that "life is too valuable for it to be endangered in the way it is by the automobile today." [44] The editor ponders on the possible constructive results accruing from such things as sentencing automobile speeders to visit hospital wards to see people maimed for life or to be led through morgues "where repose mangled bodies of several persons . . . killed by automobiles." [45]

The prophecy of Nahum,

> The chariots shall rage in the streets; they shall jostle one against another in the broad ways, they shall seem like torches, and they shall run like the lightnings, [46]

is of peculiar interest to this group. The automobile very strikingly seems to fulfill "this description to a finish, particularly the 'jostling' and the 'running like lightning.' "[47]

Graphically and tersely the group of Unitarians, speaking through the columns of its official journal, presents a listing of what might well be termed assets and liabilities of the automobile as it sees them. The ledger runs thus:

> The automobile has passed from the luxury into the necessary class. It marks the passing of an old era and the coming of a new. Its daily use adds to the joy of multitudes, and it has tremendously speeded up business. It has so complicated criminal procedure that a new body of laws has been found necessary. It has sent families all over the country into bankruptcy. It has paved the way for youthful escapades of questionable results and disastrous intrigues. [48]

The reader is not left entirely to his own devices in arriving at the balance: "Let's keep it [the automobile] a servant, not a master!"[49]

And here again, concern over speed, accidents, and the consequent loss of life is discernible. The deadly motor traffic has brought us to a situation almost intolerable. The rate of thirty-five miles an hour permitted to country road travel is startling.[50] It seems to be laboring the obvious to remind motorists that "the best preventive to accident is reduced speed."[51] Nevertheless, drivers still continue "to tear with unreckoned speed out of side streets, pass a line of leading automobiles on a curve, [and] take sharp corners on two wheels."[52]

But the rainbow is in the sky, and opinion exults as it peers beyond the horizon and sees that

> the day is fast approaching when these criminals will be deprived of their automobiles and punished with more severity than at present, for

the rights of law-abiding drivers and helpless folk cannot wait on speed lust.[53]

Settling back to await that millennium, public sentiment muses that "it is a good thing to have a Don't-Get-Hurt week, but it is much better to have a Slow-Down-There all the year round."[54]

"Speeditis" is found to be the ailment of the day in the diagnostic examination on the automobile as Presbyterian attitude views the chart. A new weapon—the automobile—has been placed in the hands of selfish and irresponsible men and women. Well-intentioned drivers observant of rules have no chance against speed maniacs.[55] It appears that the only solution lies in the direction of stringent penalties for speeding—not merely small fines which to the wealthy are mere trifles, but rather sentences of imprisonment.

Public opinion has spoken. Its utterances lack any singular dramatic qualities—in fact, most of the sentiments might be styled "mere platitudes." However, the public has been vocal, even if not forceful, and the common denominator it sees in the social effects of the automobile is the inroad it has made on safe living. To no one denominational group has the automobile made its advent amid a thundering applause of approval. It has come and has been accepted as a mixed blessing.

Our spotlight turns—it is being focused on sports.

Riding the high tide of prosperity in the flush years of the postwar decade, American enthusiasm, ever easily incited, pitched itself high and gave vent to its verve in the field of sports. Technological improvements meant more leisure for recreation, and for many, recreation and sports became, for all practical purposes, synonymous terms.

Football, baseball, golf, prize fighting, tennis, basketball, ice hockey, swimming,—all developed rapidly, and, shot through as they were with the characteristic competitive spirit, brought to the shores of the United States many trophies, ribbons, and world championships.

In a holiday mood, the nation opened wide the gates in all avenues of life for the onward rush of sports. The Baptist denomination, in an alarmed tone, expresses consternation over the inroads thus made.

The . . . daily paper has a "Sports Section" devoted to a detailed account of the doings of the sporting world. The up-to-date department store has a "Sporting Goods Section," in which one may buy golf clubs, boxing gloves, footballs, and tennis racquets. Educators of eminence are beginning to deplore quite loudly the predominance of athletic interests in our colleges and the subordination of their major purposes to the demands of the sporting group.[56]

Looking to the religious sphere of man's life, it cannot restrain a chiding quip as it calls to task the Bishop of an Episcopal Cathedral who has expressed a desire to have a " 'Sportsman's Bay' to be filled with sculptured forms of track athletes, wrestlers, and boxers."[57] It is his belief that " 'the beautiful game of polo, in its place, is as pleasing to God as a beautiful service in a beautiful cathedral.' "[58] At this observation, the Baptist editor wonders why

> if he [the Bishop] really does so believe . . . did he not build and equip a polo field instead of soliciting millions from Jews and non-conformists to build a cathedral? It would have been quite as rewardful and not nearly so expensive.[59]

Lutherans would take issue with "the princely sums of money . . . being devoted to various sports."[60] Thinking, sober Americans have food for thought on this score.

In these years, too, sports underwent a change in themselves in so far that gradually the term "professional" was becoming prefixed to the word, bringing with it a host of complex problems. The decade was to see an ever-increasing number of players in various sports. Of this general tendency, religious leaders are keenly aware:

> The plain truth is that Americans are more and more getting their recreation by proxy . . . [for instance] baseball consists of a few hundred . . . players . . . and tens of thousands of "rooters," "fans," bench warmers, patrons. . . . Play by proxy is of no particular use in providing a sound body for the use of a sound mind.[61]

The Episcopalian segment is just as relentless.

> The professionals . . . have turned what should be recreation into gain. . . . Professionalism has spoiled . . . almost every game with the possible exception of "Old Maid," Cribbage, and "My Bird Sings." The result is that (1) People prefer looking on at games to playing them themselves. (2) They demand professionals and they bet on them. (3) Some games become so professionally perfect that people no longer care to look on them.[62]

Those who do not participate "are supposed to make up for it by responding to the lunatic contortions of 'the cheer leader,' and by

'standing back of the team.' Whether it is better to play games, even badly, or to applaud those who play them well, judge ye. . . ."[63]

The Catholic voice is likewise raised in opposition as it looks back and realizes that

> gone are the days when a laurel wreath and a pindaric ode gave the brawny champion all he cared for in this world. Rivalry and advertising value have placed upon the prospective winner's back, in far too many instances, a little sign which says—"How much am I offered?" The result is what is termed professionalism—a malady which renders it impossible to impose scholastic standards upon the heads of sporting page idols.[64]

It would delight to see public opinion remedy the situation, but admits this is probably indulging in wishful wishing for "it would seem that public opinion is fundamentally interested in the score. It may put its tongue in its cheek and speculate about the price of a team and its coach, but it comes to see and place its bets on a winning outfit. . . ."[65]

Perhaps, the game far out in front for winning popular acclaim was baseball as it moved into the position of a national sport. In 1923 a World Series drew a crowd of three hundred thousand spectators and realized gate receipts of more than a million dollars.[66] However, it does not bear its honor unchallenged.

In the first year of the decade the Unitarians make no attempt to be dispassionate in their comments on baseball to which they deny the noble title of "sport." For our game is not a sport.

> When a nation's official game in almost any city has for its principal backers and enthusiasts the cheap politician, the tin-horn gambler, and the erstwhile saloon keeper, the word "sport" is permissible only as a colloquial term to which these gentry have degraded it. It is not the real thing. . . . Baseball is not a game, either, in the pure meaning of that word.[67]

The members of this same group are ready with a possible solution, and so eager are they to rid the nation of the evils of baseball as it is being carried out that

> we could see every professional player as such become extinct forthwith. . . . We say close up the grounds, let the owners suffer losses—if there be any—like the liquor traffic to which baseball has become so closely akin, and let us increase the game by opening up more city lots.[68]

It is more than mildly surprising to note that at mid-decade, the Unitarians have well nigh deserted their former position from which the above editorial comments were forthcoming. In 1925, pondering on a recently concluded world series, this group notes, with a noticeable twinge of satisfaction, that the devotion of the American people towards sports is increasing if added space given games of all kinds in the news might be considered a criterion.[69] There is much to commend in baseball now, and this it is anxious for readers to recall when objections are tossed out.

Men who achieve distinction in athletics must observe rigid rules of health. They must practice a high degree of self-control. They must have nerves of steel. They must, above all, do that extremely difficult thing, preserve a balance when the public uproariously applauds or bitterly censures.[70]

Yes, the American mind swings to sports. The Unitarians would even be willing to wager that pitching and batting averages are of more vital concern to sport-loving Americans than Presidential addresses brimming with wisdom.[71]

Rigorous and severe is the sentiment of the Presbyterians on the subject of baseball. Doubting the value of the game, the editor of an official periodical desires to toss out a few choice tidbits garnered from reflections on the sport. Obviously, very definite groups are intended to take notice.

Two or three hours in a ball park do not take anything off the waistline of the spectators or add anything to chest measurement.[72]

Newspaper men are reminded in another comment that professional baseball is a stimulus for boys, but journalism has overfed it with space.[73] And to all readers in general, the editorial column hurries on to announce—with incentive enough to produce public action— that "amateur sports seldom produce the ability of professional sports, but they produce sound citizenry."[74]

Like The Christian Register, The Presbyterian Banner, after a few years of the decade have rolled by, gives indications of attempting to soft-pedal previous objections. The effort, however, is only halfhearted, and 1927 finds the Presbyterians still wondering "if it is not about time there should be some reaction against the excessive craze for sports."[75]

Some abuse of "trades" and the open sale and barter of players reported in sport columns of daily papers call forth regret on the part of the Catholics, for whom *The Commonweal* speaks, that the sport should be thus besmirched. Catholic opinion is notably reticent on the existing or supposedly existing evils of baseball, and in commenting on the same world series and in much the same complacent accents as the Unitarian contemporaries did, it feels sure that "the curves and . . . smashes into the vista of world news during the playing of the series show . . . how firm a nucleus for our thoughts and emotions is afforded by the national game."[76]

The Lutherans beg to differ with all whose sentiments are of like color with those above. "As for ourselves, we do not view this temporary baseball insanity without alarm."[77] In fact, the unfavorable criticism passed on our American civilization from many quarters is deservedly merited.

> That a series of baseball games should for an entire month furnish conversation to millions; that the home-coming of the pennant winners should unloosen such floods of enthusiasm as a city used to accord to heroes returning from war; that even business, that sacred institution, should come to a standstill in several great American cities while the contest was going on—these have tarnished the nation's escutcheon.[78]

"When 10,000 stand in line in order to obtain a ticket for a crucial 'World Series' game, we cannot suppress the wish that men would seek with the same eagerness the preaching of the eternal Gospel."[79]

"It is the old story of temptation and a fall," the Baptists believe, that is responsible for the base in baseball. Gamblers not only corrupt the game but also the players—but, on second thought, if "[the players] were not gamblers at heart and in practice they could not be tempted."[80] In a continuing tone of carping and caustic criticism, this section questions the value of "Babe" Ruth to organized baseball. Is he, whose salary goes "in the class with the President of the United States" as useful a citizen of the world and of the Kingdom of God as a man receiving many times less that salary?

> He certainly is not. Is baseball a real man's job in a world as disturbed as ours? Some will say that anybody who helps to keep others interested and happy is doing a real service. Others will make the same comment we [desire to make]: "Few things look so shiftless as a big, strong, full-grown man selling pop." [81]

The conscience of the Methodist group is disturbed by the disconcerting but nonetheless well-founded information that "there is a great deal of gambling in connection with the sport."[82] Bribery and dishonesty in America's greatest national sport has besmirched the reputation of the game, but can "a sport or other institution that fosters gambling [be] worthy of a clean 'reputation'?"[83]

Running a close second with baseball for first place in popularity was football. It was and remained essentially a college game, but in the Twenties it kicked its way into the hearts of an ever-increasing number of followers,[84] and stadia, sometimes of a size to accommodate seventy or eighty thousand spectators, sprang up all over the country.

Football of the 1920's was a new game not only on the score of altered rules. Previously, it had been of interest chiefly to students and alumni; now it attracted the general public. New, too, was it in that whereas former complaints had been brought against the brutality of the game, now charges that an amateur sport was being transformed into a commercial amusement business run by coaches and alumni for the benefit of the general sporting public were leveled against it.[85]

Certain religious groups—Catholics, Methodists, Unitarians, and Presbyterians—expressing opinion in the columns of their periodicals used in this study,—unite voices in a chorus of protest against the obvious and disintegrating effects of football, as it was then being played, on American youth.

The adamant tone of the Catholic section represented by the *America* is pronounced. Its language is pointed and detailed, as it comments on a *Bulletin of the American Association of University Professors* recently published relative to college sports.

Two great disadvantages of college football are first, over-excitement prevailing through the autumn, second, the consequent distortion of values obtaining throughout the year. This over-excitement rises in the case of final games into what we are told "is fairly to be designated as hysteria." It is fanned into absurd flames at "pep sessions" and bursts into its culmination in "the madness of the yelling mob at the game itself." Negligence in study is noted as an accompanying consequence. But the second great disadvantage . . . the distortion of values, lasts throughout the college course, if not through life. A hero worship of football prowess, not of personal excellence, is bad. Again, the huge financial aspect of football and the tempting salary to the player who will turn professional unsettle ideas and ideals. . . . Appreciation of intellectual training and desire for academic distinction are attenuated and future leaders in human society are lost.[86]

Other disadvantages hardly less secondary than the preceding ones, such as drinking, encouragement of betting, and provocation of dishonesty are noted.

As far as the group behind the columns of *The Commonweal* is concerned, there is a favorable aspect of the game that cannot be completely ignored.

> Football almost deprives autumn of its melancholy title. The high spirits so cheerfully expended on the gridiron seem to inoculate everybody with germs of hilarity and enthusiasm which triumphantly combat, for the moment at least, the morose infections of business and society.[87]

Nevertheless, the reverse side of the same coin is more sinister than some care to believe. The game is receiving the wrong sort of emphasis in colleges, most of it originating far from the ivy lanes of the campus.

> Generally it is the alumni who promote the demand for huge and expensive stadia, for a small army of coaches and other attendants, and for a hundred other methods of spending money, and of distracting the attention of the student from the real work of the college.[88]

The group of Catholics is willing to exonerate the college players themselves of real guilt for it is the older generation who clamors for winning teams and stoops to methods that are decidedly suspicious in enlisting promising high school players, and who prefers a coach who can produce a winning team to a coach who teaches that there can be something better in the game than victory.[89]

Football, already tainted, is made still more ominous by the entrance of the professional. "He has introduced the system of providing certain players with private press agents to keep these boys in the public eye during the football season, thereby enhancing the value when he enlists them for his professional teams."[90] The public sense of devotion to ideals of truth and honor ought to be aroused by these violations.

With many of their contemporaries, the Methodists of the Southern Conference are ready and willing to subscribe to the rightful place of athletics in school life. The group agrees that sports can and should contribute to exercise, sportsmanship, and student acquaintance. Play is valuable. But intercollegiate games may become harmful. In fact, they often exceed all bounds of propriety.[91] And today the athletic activities of the college are doing just that. They have become, in large measure, professional both in method and in organization and now hold first place in the interest of both students and the public. "The paid coach and the professional organization of college athletics, the demoralization of students by participation in the use of extravagant sums of money, constitute a reproach to American colleges and to those who govern them."[92]

"What a pity," is the regretful comment the same group makes as it reviews the lack of appreciation of values that athletics have engendered even among administration members. Quoting from another Methodist publication, it declares:

> The professor in Greek gets $3,000 salary, and the football coach in the same college receives $12,000. This discrepancy can be explained in that 50,000 cheer a football game while not a solitary mortal cheers a Greek recitation. Nevertheless, it is a striking instance of misplaced values. For Homer's *Illiad* is of infinitely greater worth than any story of the Olympic games. The glories of ancient Greece rest upon art and literature and not upon athletics. Modern colleges are in grave danger of becoming huge athletic associations.[93]

The theme of protest woven into the complaints of the Unitarians is not different from that of the above two sections of religious groups. Usually very "liberal" in outlook, the Unitarians, in this instance, are of a mind to take their place with others who oppose paid players in football.

> There is more professionalism in college teams today than there ever was, according to information which we gather and believe. Graduate athletic managers and even responsible faculty members know that all varieties of crookedness are permitted and encouraged. . . . It is safe to say that every considerable college in the land is tainted.[94]

The Presbyterians, in commenting on a *Bulletin of the American Association of University Professors*—the same issue that provoked the ire of the Catholic segment[95]—commit themselves to the condemnation of college football as it is at the moment. In itself the game is "a good sport and an interesting sport, which properly limited and controlled, by its recreative values, helps and not hinders the attaining of the central intellectual purpose of the college."[96] A severe arraignment against the over-excitement, distortion of values, incitement to drinking and dishonesty is practically of the same pattern as that of the Catholic sentiment on the same aspects.

Speaking generally, with one eye on the above reproachful incriminations that have befallen college football in the opinion of religious denominational groups, sentiment seems to have crystallized on two evils, namely, its overshadowing of intellectual pursuits, and its professionalism with the attendant vices.

Next to a world series baseball game that drew crowds which would do honor to a Presidential inauguration ceremony, or a football match with its pageantry of "gay colors in the stands, the organized cheering under specially drilled cheer leaders, the military parade of the college band, the tense atmosphere of suspense when seventy thousand clamorous voices were hushed as a pigskin hesitated in mid-air above the wooden crossbar,"[97] prize fighting attracted the next largest number of spectators to its ringside.

On July 4, 1919, Jack Dempsey gained the heavyweight title in a bout with Jess Willard, and on that occasion the new champion injected into the sport an indefinable "something" which catapulted the game, almost overnight, into a national favorite. However, it did not mount to its decorous position without much opposition. Presbyterians, Methodists, and Lutherans were on the offensive at once.

In 1921, *The Presbyterian Banner*, reeling under the blow of a recent fight in which Mr. Dempsey defeated a French challenger, Georges Carpentier, feels that the time has come to speak. This bout drew gate receipts of over a million and a half dollars.

On the first count, its voice is raised against the gambling activities that went on in connection with the contest. "It was so large as to suggest that we are a nation of gamblers, and that gambling is a legitimate business."[98] Notwithstanding the fact that there were many who "did not bow the knee to this Baal," a second count must be called against the sport in that it calls forth almost general interest and approval. It is a matter of deep concern how we can "go wild over a prize fight" and at the same time talk about our high Christian ideals. Truth is

> we are following the example of Rome, when it hastened its own downfall by its gladiatorial shows, when more than a quarter of a million people would assemble to witness a conflict between gladiatorial slaves, or perchance see a Nubian lion rush upon and devour Christian men and women. It may not be popular to say so; nevertheless we are

compelled to say that this whole business seems distressing and disgusting to us, and utterly unworthy of Christian America. If dogfights, bullfights, and all classes of prize fights were left to the plug-uglies and to the rabble it would not be so discouraging.[99]

In 1927 when what was perhaps the most highly publicized sports spectacle of the decade, the second Tunney-Dempsey fight at Chicago, recorded gate receipts of over two and a half million dollars, the Presbyterians again found it impossible to maintain silence. Again, as six years earlier, thoughts stray back to days long past but replete with instruction for the present. "They opened a Roman Colosseum in Chicago last week and twice as many frenzied people witnessed the brutal spectacle as looked down upon the bloodstained sand of the Roman arena."[100] Whether the votaries of this degrading exhibition be governors or socialites, the sport is not a respectable one. "The glorification of the animal and sensual . . . is a grave symptom in our modern world."[101] Can one help wondering if "we are going pleasure-mad and smothering the spirit in the flesh as Rome did when tottering to its fall?"[102]

"The good old days" impinge on the memory of Baptist opinion as it recalls that "before the war there were few places in the United States where a professional prize fight could be held. We should get back to the old standard. There is no room for being proud of the liberty which allows bruising exhibitions of the kind which are now becoming too common."[103] Various contests, other than those which called forth denunciations from the Presbyterian group, come under fire here. The first one was a fight held early in 1925 in Madison Square Garden.

Two young brutes . . . fought nine rounds of a fifteen round battle and then one of them, pounded to a pulp under the fury and driving force of the other's blows, had to give up. A crowd of 9,530 people looked on, and paid $33,967 to see the degenerate exhibition. We venture that hardly a dozen of them would have given even a dollar to any really good cause. Such a show gathers together the worst of every bad class in the community.[104]

The following year the Sesquicentennial Exhibition held in Philadelphia gave proof secure to this denomination that the unholy partnership of the world, the flesh and the devil, had scored another triumph. The authorities "defied God by desecrating the Lord's Day" in opening gates to the Fair Grounds on Sunday, and "now we hear

that the pagan management is to stage a prize fight between two
lusty brutes in order to get more money to support their show."[105]
It is deplorable that the mayor of the city, "a putty-faced temporizer
who can be relied upon in nothing,"[106] panders to the lowest element
in the community.
At the close of the decade, another bout called forth thundering
opposition.

> We listened in the other night as Mr. Graham McNamee broad-
> casted the details of the Sharkey-Stribling fight at Miami, Florida. It
> was disgusting enough as reported to fill us with shame. Yet 35,000
> people—including high public officials and many society men and
> women—sat beside the ring and enjoyed seeing the blood spurt.[107]

The Madison Square Garden contest and the Sesquicentennial
Fair likewise drew withering comments from the Methodist publication. The fact that the bout in New York had been promoted by a
daughter of J. Pierpont Morgan for the relief of devastated France in
no manner justifies the disgraceful contest—in fact, devastating
America in the name of charity cries to heaven for vengeance.

> The disgusting spectacle in the ring was nothing to what went on
> outside. Young girls from the "first families" sold programs and Miss
> Morgan herself . . . sat in a box with ex-Governor Smith and smiled
> her thanks to the cheering thousands. . . . Prize fighting levels the
> fighters to brutes, and its effect on the spectators is scarcely less de-
> basing. The man or woman who promotes such an exhibition starts an
> endless train of debasing influences. When that man or woman is not
> a plug-ugly, but a member of a family which has at least the opportunity
> of refinement and Christian culture, the case is far more deplorable.[108]

And the Sesquicentennial has brought disgrace on the City of
Brotherly Love by desecrating the Sunday, but this outrage was not
the limit.

> The high point in the program of Philadelphia's celebration of the
> signing of the Declaration of Independence . . . is not to be the visit of
> the President, but a prize fight for the heavyweight championship of
> these States of right free and independent. Jack Dempsey displaces
> Calvin Coolidge as the Fair's prime attraction. The Sesquicentennial
> stadium offers the largest prize ring in America, and more men and
> women will pay to see two brutes slug each other while the rest of
> America, with itching ears, picks the fight out of the air. . . . When

Tex Rickard's resources as a drawer of gate-money to the Sesquicentennial Fair have been exhausted, there still remains Earl Carroll![109]

The first fight between Jack Dempsey and Gene Tunney in 1926, which attracted a crowd of 67,000 spectators, is beyond the pale of clean sports in the opinion of the Lutheran group comprising the Missouri Synod. It can find "nothing uplifting about two beefy specimens of humanity pounding each other around the prize ring."[110]

The official organ speaking for the United Lutherans is inclined to think that by and large "the sentiment of the country (outside of certain sporting elements who revel in cockfights, dogfights, bullfights, and manfights) is against brutalizing sports."[111] However, the opposition must become more vocal. It is a travesty on the nation's sense of decency to allow the responsibility of creating the sentiment of protest to devolve upon the pulpit and the religious press. So blatant an offense as fighting should arouse every rightthinking citizen.[112]

One is led to surmise that the editor is speaking with his tongue in his cheek as he recounts an incident. A Lutheran pastor sent to the editorial office a clipping of a Roman Catholic priest quoting him as approving of boxing in the parish hall after services, and hoping it would not be frowned upon. Incidentally, results, too, were gratifying: the church was well-filled. The editor quickly adds that the report may be a misstatement, but actually thinks this is what is happening in fact. "In an almost frantic effort to draw them to the Church, not only Roman Catholic priests, but Protestant preachers as well, seem to deem it necessary to introduce sports of various kinds to keep young people interested. Interested in what? In religion? No, not in religion, but in sports. . . . O tempora! O mores!"[113]

Preoccupation with Football, Baseball, and Prize fighting apparently dwarfed the importance of other sports in the public mind. Other than a few meager allusions to golf in so far as it intruded on the sanctity of the Sunday on the part of Baptists and Presbyterians, there seems to have been no protest reaction to the other games in which Americans were making merry.[114] Of course, it should be recalled that Football, Baseball, and Prize fighting were unique, too, in that they captured the national consciousness as no other sport did.

The years of the Twenties have often been termed a "Roman holiday"—and not too inapt does the phrase seem as one leafs the years of that decade. There seemed to be bread aplenty, and avidly the people were looking for circuses. Someone has wisely remarked that anyone who wanted to lead a peaceful life picked the wrong era in which to live if he chose this postwar period. Speeding and sporting were not by any means the only attractions; in fact, they were only two of a host of distractions.

Novel in itself, the period was most cordial to change, to anything savoring of what was untried and free from conventionality. In their holiday spirit many Americans of the 1920's were in the mood to wind up the red tape of tradition and to drink deeply the draughts of "freedom." Restraining voices of various groups might cry out—but these were little more than cries in the wilderness. In such an intellectual climate as the Twenties provided, it is thus comparatively easy to account for the undue interest evinced in what might be termed "the spectacular." In this area, the religious press will again be found reproving, entreating, rebuking.

The ancient Athenians, with whom Paul tried to reason, the Lutherans declare, could not have had more itching ears to hear things new and strange and fanciful and abnormal than our American youth.

> The drift away from that which has been tried and found true is reflected in the novelties and oddities over which so many of even our supposedly well-educated youth become enamoured. That is why as a people we are fast becoming freakish and eccentric.[115]

Liberty is so misconstrued that, for many, it symbolizes nothing but the rupture of all attachments to what is normal, sensible, and stable. Finer tastes and nobler ideals are being shattered by the craze for abnormality.

> No doubt every age has had its weaklings who are fond of freaks and oddities; but just now we seem to be suffering from an epidemic of this disease. With all our boasted education we seem to be developing a race of literacy degenerates who mistake eccentricity for high art and who have about as much ethical sense as the ape from whom man is supposed to have sprung. They sometimes make us feel that there is better evidence for believing that man is descending to the ape rather than that he has descended from him.[116]

Indeed, "absurdities never cease," muses the editor of the official publication of the Episcopalians with a nod of assent. "Freak" weddings are widespread. Young people seek novel means of getting married in order to shock their friends. And, sad to relate, the couple that wants to be married "in a balloon or on roller skates has no difficulty in finding a parson to tie the knot."[117] Variations of "freak" or "mock" weddings are almost as numerous as the famous fifty-seven varieties. One recently was composed of men exclusively and termed "The Womanless Wedding,"—suggestive of Neronian horrors.[118] Another account tells of a bridegroom being kidnapped and carried through the town in a "police patrol wagon as a prisoner," escorted by a jazz band.[119] A preacher in the mid-West was subjected to a disgrace at his own wedding. Friends abducted him, screwed him into a coffin, and carried him to a neighboring town. There his new wife was also brought on a motor truck. The couple were reunited in jail, and then released.[120]

Another "freak" has made its appearance.

A baptism [took place] on a steel girder fourteen stories high down in New Orleans. The child of a structural ironworker was carried aloft for that purpose, while his father's trade union associates, perched on the skeleton of the building, were sponsors.[121]

The periodical does not know what sort of minister performed the rite, but it does know that he, as well as the parents, needs instruction in the elements of reverence and common sense.[122]

The "Ouija Board drivel" solicits a comment from the Reform Jewish section.

During the first year of the war, men and women took to reading Bibles and going to church, and . . . during the second and subsequent years they bought Ouija boards and began going to mediums. . . . One look at the . . . vacuous, semi-idiotic expression of a man or woman playing the Ouija game is enough to convince an unimpassioned spectator with the truth of Puck's immortal dictum, "What fools ye mortals be!" [123]

With a tone of contemptuous ridicule, the Baptists deflate the frenzied enthusiasm for daft publicity stunts—this time, flagpole-sitting.

Grabbing notoriety is getting to be a great game. Sitting on top of a high flagpole a number of days is a device chosen by ludicrous individuals to make the people gape.[124]

With the usual stock of sensations running stale, the denomination wonders if this enterprise may not be turned to account in evangelism. The tone of the suggestion cannot be missed.

> To the variegated but familiar aggregation of oddities might be added the "Steeple Jack Evangelist," who preaches every day standing on top of the highest flagpole in the neighborhood. If the evangelist should be a woman the effect would be enhanced.[125]

The progress of aviation during the early years of the 1920's was outstanding. Records for speed and endurance, which today seem very unimpressive, were being constantly broken. The first triumphant round-the-world flight was made in 1924, and three years later, Charles A. Lindbergh made his sensational trans-Atlantic flight. After this, public interest in long-distance flying and its possibilities became intense. However, it is obvious from editorial comment that enthusiasm in so-called "stunt" flying was alive and keen throughout the span of the decade.

In 1920, Methodists of the Southern Conference, in their official publication, quote and acquiesce with a Presbyterian journal which comments rather caustically on the recent death of a "stunt flyer." The fate of the reckless young aeronaut will not, unfortunately, prevent others from emulating him.

> Common sense should be sufficient to prevent cities, amusement parks, etc., from having men to imperil their lives by hair-raising feats to furnish thrills to a gaping morbid throng of people; but since it is not, there should be a law preventing a man from imperiling his life in an adventure which could serve no useful end.[126]

Two years later, with no evident abatement of what they call the "Flying Circus" the Methodists again voice their opinion. In July, an aviator, in attempting to swing from one plane to another by means of a "ropy ladder" was killed in the endeavor. This religious group would say that a flyer who acts the part of a daredevil to thrill gaping sight-seers is "serving the real devil."[127]

Again in September of 1922, when four airmen lost their lives at an Eastern fair while performing, the admonition comes that "no man has any moral right to endanger his life to entertain the gaping thousands."[128] Such feats make one wonder how far our civilization is in retrogression.

In olden days Romans had their gladiatorial sports. We regard such sport as worse than barbarous and hold up our hands in horror to think that thousands and thousands of men and women in Rome's high day would gather to see men cut each other to pieces in the gladiatorial ring. Are we any better when we turn out to watch men take their lives in their own hands in performing feats in the air?[129]

The unjustifiable risks taken by flyers are in no manner to be condoned, but the group for whom *The Watchman-Examiner* speaks, thinks it might be well to declare that "old-fashioned people [ought] to realize that the mode of travel by air is not responsible for the folly of . . . men and women who do 'stunt' flights."[130]

The first woman to swim the English Channel was a nineteen year old girl, Gertrude Ederle, of New York. Characteristic of the spirit of 1926 was the reception Miss Ederle received on her return to New York where her ship was met by an official yacht, circling planes, and a Fire Department band. Fifteen thousand people turned out to welcome her. The representative of the mayor of the city likened her exploit to Moses' crossing of the Red Sea and Caesar's crossing of the Rubicon. Regardless of how similar to historical incidents her success was, certain it is that her feat was a springboard for many others to attempt similar deeds. The fondness for publicity has gripped sport-loving Americans to such a degree that they will even welcome fictitious notoriety, is the opinion of the Presbyterian segment. "The business [of swimming feats] is a bid for notoriety. It is part of the craze for cheap publicity . . . leading some to attempt the . . . useless feat of swimming the English Channel. The latest woman to enter this competition faked the whole business, riding most of the way in a boat."[131] Perhaps the public would do well to cease exploiting those who do these things and let them pass into the obscurity from which they emerged.[132]

Another new American sensation caught the public eye during the summer of 1921—the bathing beauty. In early July a Costume and Beauty Show was held on a bathing beach along the Potomac River in Washington. Various cities soon followed suit, and in early September, the various state winners assembled in Atlantic City for a national contest. This exploiting and commercializing of feminine beauty summons forth the ire of the Lutherans.

We are invited to pay tribute to silly girls who have by accident inherited pretty faces. Much is made of the woman who happens to have an almost perfect physique, often displayed in total defiance of modesty and decency. It seems to have become quite a fad to conduct contests in cities in order to ascertain who is "the prettiest girl in town." Then the contest enlarges and these beauties are summoned to some resort like Atlantic City to put themselves on exhibition in scant seashore garb and have judges decide to whom the prize for supremest beauty should be awarded, very much as birds and fowls and cattle are exhibited at the county fairs and passed upon.[133]

Some of the young girls who have been favored with attractive forms and faces may be led into beauty contests thoughtlessly and innocently, but this religious denominational group wonders why there has been no loud and insistent outcry against this unprincipled practice. Much has been said in condemnation of it by individuals and by church papers and associations here and there. What is needed is concerted effort to create public sentiment against it.[134]

Unseemly and debasing are apt descriptives in the minds of Presbyterians for these "bathing beauty contests that have now spread over the country and wind up at Atlantic City in a public parade to be stared at by ogling eyes."[135] This religious group is convinced that

> no right-thinking, self-respecting woman should be willing to exhibit and expose herself in this way for the low price of a little cheap notoriety. Even in the display of their own line of goods these young women, judged by their published pictures, are disappointing, and some of them appear to be as meagerly endowed with beauty as they are scantily supplied with clothing. The whole thing is vulgar and debasing.[136]

Marathons, another one of "the spectaculars" in the Twenties,— be they in dancing or running—suggest themselves to both Lutherans and Baptists for appraisal, and with resulting judgments that are highly surprising.

Originating in the British Isles, Dance Marathons were shortly imported into the United States. The first contest was held March 31, 1923. For a while the vogue for the contests was remarkable. In June, 1928, a $5,000 prize meet was held at Madison Square Garden in New York.

Lutherans consider that "the participating of morons, half-wits, and nit-wits" in the "long-distance dance" may be a "symptom of mental breakdown, the result of overindulgence in that hideous shuffling and squirming of men and women locked in close embrace called the modern dance."[137] An effective description presented for reader consumption is an account of an eyewitness: "I . . . saw them dragging and carrying out the dancers, as they collapsed, hollow-eyed, sunken-cheeked, hair and clothes untidied, etc. I have seen many a down-and-out but this scene eclipsed them all."[138] Let us drop the curtain on this odious business!

Unitarians, considering dancing a legitimate method of relaxation and enjoyment, ordinarily do not proscribe it.

> But when young couples dance continuously seventy and eighty hours in the attempt to make records; when they perform such insane feats as to dance the limit of one State, dance into a taxicab, continue to dance while the cab is going to the ferry, dance out and onto the ferryboat, dance on the boat, while it is crossing the river to another State, dance into a taxicab on the farther shore, and so on to the dancehalls in the other State . . . it is time to enter a vigorous protest.[139]

In 1925, Paavo Nurmi, called the "Flying Finn" came to the United States and showed an astonished crowd that it was possible to run two miles in less than nine minutes. Thereafter, the American track posed possibilities for lovers of what was spectacular.

One is at first glance astonished at *The Watchman-Examiner's* exultant shout of "Hats off" to the winner of a Running Marathon in 1927. A second glance assures him that enthusiasm is grounded on fact. The new champion, "a Yankee hero of the Baptist persuasion," is a man "of the highest Christian principles and has been for years a teacher in the Baptist Sunday School."[140] Recalling the Epistle to the Hebrews, the Baptist group feels that "perhaps . . . the vigor and endurance which gave him Marathon victories are due to the fact that he has practiced day by day [the] running [of] the fine and wholesome Race of Righteousness."[141]

At this point, let us step back and allow the Lutherans, with deft skill, to write the epitome.

> What strange heroes the masses today are worshipping! A fighter who has won his laurels in the ring moves from city to city with countless throngs to hail him, such as kings might well covet. A base-ball or football player who has reached the highest peak of perfection in his art, a woman tennis player who expects to pocket a hundred thousand dollars or more by putting her art on exhibition, or a doughty girl . . . who swims the English Channel, or a pretty maiden who wins the beauty prize in a national contest, seem to catch the imagination

of Americans and turns them into ardent worshippers. All the best, the noblest servants of humanity who live and labor for something that is worthwhile and pleasing to God must be content to pass unnamed, unhonored, and unsung.[142]

"There is a time to dance
and a time to mourn."

—*Eccl.* 3, 4.

CHAPTER VI

The Dancing Daze

Out from the deep recesses of the long-buried past, sounds a clarion note—arresting, apropos. "There is a time to dance and a time to mourn."[1] Then, in the decade of the 1920's, if ever, the inspired writer's dictum touched responsive chords. On the part of youth, the era was assuredly one in which to dance. As for the mourning, that might well be left to others, who, incidentally, were doing just that.

In these days, amusements of all types gripped the hearts of pleasure-loving Americans, and, of the less strenuous amusements, dancing was the chief attraction. There was really nothing new about dancing. Throughout the ages it had appealed to all men. Imitation and emulation of King David, who danced with all his might, were not reserved for the Twenties. However, never before had this ancient and natural amusement been forced through such rapid changes.

New and different dances replaced the older, sedate, reserved forms, and dancing academies by the score appeared to draw patronage from youth anxious to master the intricacies of new fashions in dancing steps. In the home, in the church, in the school, everywhere there was dancing.

The type of music supposedly characteristic of the era was jazz. It spread with the new dances and each urged the other to fresh triumphs. Paul Whiteman, often dubbed "King of Jazz," baffled as to defining it as a disease, art, manner, or dance, aptly described it as "the folk music of the machine age."[2]

This "music" with its erratic syncopation seemed a chaos of ugliness to ears accustomed to the suave and melodious Viennese waltzes. But as something exotic, original, and interesting, if not beautiful, in the United States its rule was as wide as the art of the dance.

Dancing and, at times, its jazz musical accompaniment were received with ill-concealed hostility by the majority of the religious groups, and subjected to endless denunciations. In 1926, when Mr. Paul Whiteman asked that jazz be admitted to an honored place among the major arts, *The Commonweal* sees in his demand a portent of the mad age in which we live.

> Jazz is popular, jazz is powerful, jazz makes a great deal of money and is the idol of the country in which most of the money is made. Like many another thing that is rich, powerful, and popular, it dislikes having its disreputable origins recalled, and its devotees are naturally angry when authentic musicians refuse to admit the parvenu to their company.[3]

"Rendering Shakespeare acceptable to the masses by rewriting him in the language of a New York Eastsider" is what jazz does to classical music, in the opinion of a music critic cited by the same Catholic group.

The Lutherans of both groups represented in this study take an unyielding position in the camp of the opposition, but nevertheless, they want all to know "it is not our intention to be joy killers."[4]

> We want our young people to drink and to drink deep of real joys . . . to have a genuine good time, but we know of a far, far better draught than that filthy and poisonous cup which the devil would raise to their lips. If we warn them against certain pleasures, it is because we know them to be the baited traps of their most bitter foes.[5]

Because of the revolting character of the modern dance—"this training school for fornication, this revolting eructation from the brothel"[6]—one is reluctant to speak out on the subject.

> First the waltz, then the tango, then the turkey trot, the fox trot, and the one-step, and now the final abomination, the shimmy dance. One hates to mention these more recent public stimulations of fleshy desire . . . even by name.[7]

Old dances were objectionable only because they were sources of temptation to sin. The modern dance is no longer temptation; "it is undeniably indulgence in fleshly lust. . . ."[8] This evil has assumed proportions that

> the warning "not to be conformed to the world" must now be emphasized with special reference to these seductions lest our young

people (and their elders, too) be seared in their conscience through indulgence in them and be ruined in soul and body.[9]

However, the group feels that it is entirely useless to warn the vicious against dancing. Rather it is "the heedless and inexperienced young Christian who imagines his elders and his pastor wish to interfere with the . . . good time of young people."[10]

The problem is definitely a complex one, but the solution that some parents and teachers are suggesting, namely, the hiring of an approved dancing master with weekly dances conducted under supervision, is far afield of an effective answer. Approved dancing professors and genteel chaperones will never make dancing of any kind a safe proposition.[11]

> Will [parents and teachers] never learn that thousands upon thousands of girls that were once pure are now in the houses of ill repute because they took their first steps in some select parlor dance? These dances, wherever they may be held, are designed to kindle the passions of young men. Whether in parlor, school, or public hall, the thought-life of any young man is almost certain to be set on fire of hell.[12]

The music of the day also poses some food for pondering souls. The devil, aware that music is powerful but subtle in influence, gradual and illusive in effects, may use jazz as a wedge into homes, schools, and social circles. "The reformation of music can come only by the preaching of the Gospel."[13] In all things, let young people keep their amusements "in accordance with the Word of the Best Friend of young people: 'Let everything be done decently and in order.' "[14]

The other group of the same denomination, in its official journal, in terms as pungent, expresses its opinion on the evils of the modern dance, at whose feet must be laid the blame for the frightful increase in moral wrecks among our American youth.

> It has rightly been called "the dance of death." . . . The sex intoxication, brought on by the close-grip dance, which is today the one great outstanding social enticement among all the young people of America— this snaky thing is new to the world. . . . The crux of the problem is the white heat sex stimulation which is involved.[15]

It is becoming a prevalent notion that girls are doomed to be

> beautiful wallflowers unless they doff them [corsets]. . . . It is not difficult to guess why boys do not care to dance with "old ironsides,"

and why some girls like that particular style of dance which bans corsets. Volumes could be written on this question. Its seriousness cannot be overstated.[16]

This new twentieth century dance of dances is a matter beyond the power of an individual parent to handle effectively. Only the concerted and vigorous co-operation of the home, school, church, and community at large will prove equal to the difficult task of readjustment of the sex dance.[17]

Perhaps it may be that six years later, after viewing the failure of "concerted effort" advocated by them in 1921 to meet the problem of the dance, this same group finds that the church has had to stand alone in the fight, and now it wonders if

> the Church as such [should] attempt to regulate the amusements of youth and act as censor or regulator. It would have its hands more than full. . . . It must always create sentiment against excesses or abuses; but why do not Christians and parents who favor dancing step in . . . and throw needed safeguards around it?[18]

The Methodists, during the early years of the decade, were busy with a problem peculiarly their own relative to dancing. Gathering the threads from editorial columns during the time, a pattern of their difficulty may be woven rather easily.

The National Association of Masters of Dancing, after charging the Methodist Church with hampering dancing teachers in elevating the dance, finally addressed an appeal to the General Conference asking co-operation " 'to improve the dance rather than maintain the ban which few members obey.' " In an effort to placate the Methodists, it seems that the dancing masters merely added insult to injury by naming a dance in memory of John Wesley, "Wesleyan." The Methodists met the conciliatory efforts with contempt.

> Too bad the Methodists should be so behind the times and so unappreciative! But we are inclined to think that if only "a few Church members obey the law" the dancing masters would not be so disturbed. In their agitation of the question they bear testimony to the success of the Methodists.[19]

A Baptist contemporary publication cannot contain its mirth at the announcement of the launching of the "Wesleyan."

> It reads somewhat like an extract from one of the "funny papers." . . . All objectionable features are said to have been eliminated and

the posture and movements of the dancers made entirely correct. . . .
It is now said that the association has withdrawn its new dance in
umbrage, being unable to understand the coldness of the Methodist
leaders. Funny, isn't it? Imagine John Wesley leading off in the dance
bearing his name![20]

The "withdrawal in umbrage" refers to the Dancing Masters'
Association's giving up the dance. The announcement, as quoted
in the Methodist journal, runs thus:

The dance was a very graceful one, showing the proper position of
the dancers and created to meet the approval of the most rigid Church
member; but our effort was misinterpreted, and unfortunately, the
people we were trying to win over to our side were further antagonized,
and additional attacks upon dancing followed. In view of this we have
withdrawn the "Wesleyan" and for the present will take no further
action in trying to win our religious antagonists.[21]

The Methodists themselves feel that this announcement betrays a
gross misconception of "what not only our Church but Christianity
stands for."[22] Since the dancing masters have given up the Methodists, it is up to the Methodists to reform the dance by devising some
form of "mutual athletics that will save all that is harmless and
provide all that is lacking for the social life of the young people of
both sexes."[23]

Let the incorrigible and impenitent Methodist Church reform the
dance altogether!

Hamlet instructs the players how to improve the play: "I hope,"
says the leader, "we have reformed that indifferently." "O reform it
altogether," says Hamlet.[24]

During the course of the argument, the Board of Bishops of the
Methodist Episcopal Church, according to newspaper accounts, had
barred dancing teachers from membership in the Church. The Jewish
segment speaking in this study has some comments both on this action which it considered extremely ill-timed, and on the attitude of
the Methodists towards dancing in general. "The attitude of this sect
towards amusements of any sort is too well known to need exposi-
tion."[25] In taking the step of banning teachers of dancing, it has
apparently not taken into consideration some perilous implications.
Jewish opinion is inclined "to side altogether with the amusement
people" who have expressed "indignation at what can only be

termed as a pharisaic attitude on the part of any Christian denomination."[26]

In 1923, the Methodists are still in a tangle over the same problem, but by this date they disclaim the charge that dancing teachers have ever been denied membership "when they repented of teaching lasciviousness and adultery and of ruining homes and youth."[27] The way to the altar is wide open to all penitents. "Let the teachers come, forsaking their evil deeds."[28]

It is to be noted that the Methodists were not occupied solely in discussions with dancing masters to the exclusion of concern over the dangers of the dancing and jazz craze. From their own editorial desk come censorious railings. From columns of other Methodist publications maledictions on dancing are reprinted and commented upon.

In its own name, the group explains its untractable attitude on dancing in the fact that "so far as we have been able to observe the dance never makes those participating in it more virtuous, more worthy citizens, or more Christlike in character."[29] A four months' investigation of dance halls in a large city makes unpleasant reading and

a delineation of the immorality and crime that infests them cannot be brought into these columns. . . . Methodism's protest against promiscuous dancing has never been a mistake, and Methodism needs to make her protesting voice heard now as never before.[30]

The devil and the dance are in alliance to ruin souls, and those who engage in dancing may be sure they are doing Satan's work. A little story, the editor judges, may not be out of place. According to report, the devil broke up some dancing parties by appearing in the person of someone who had on a costume equipped with electric batteries so as to give the effect of fire. The editor is not concerned as to the truth or falsity of the story, as such; but it does misinterpret and misrepresent the devil as he is.

We never yet knew the devil to try to scare folks who were serving him efficiently. So long as people are engaged in that which results in sending souls to perdition, so long as they do his work, the devil flatters and consoles them.[31]

Jazz, too, is a vice eating at the very vitals of our culture. This form of entertainment is a serious menace to our taste in music and must be driven out by the invasion of culture. Singing only tuneful melodies from the great operas is said to have made the Italian people a nation of musicians. What are we as a nation singing?[32]

Summoning other publications to the fray, the official journal siphons off some pointed editorial comments and reproduces them for popular consumption and reflection. One editor, dining in a fashionable hotel, was brought face to face with a modern custom of dancing between courses. The dances were all "the jazz kind—all dissolute and immoral. The music, too, was debasing and sensuous in its appeal."[33] Disclaiming to be a "religious fanatic" the editor had to confess "that every drop of Christian blood in my veins boiled with righteous indignation"[34] at this scene.

Borrowing from another exchange, the journal agrees that rudeness, nudeness, and lewdness are the three things that all too often accompany the modern dance. The dance, in fact, is the finishing school for these three things.

> If one wishes to become an adept in them, he can find no finer training school than the dance. We are not saying that everyone who enters these dances comes out a finished product in these three notorious attributes, but some do, and all may. We advise those who would be possessed of refined manners and moral decency to stay shy of the dance.[35]

Convinced that "jazz" music and "jazz" dancing are mightily out of place in the White House, a clipping from a Washington paper telling of a dance in which the President took part is distressing in its content.

> We do not think it comports with the dignity of his high office, for the President of the United States to engage in such frivolous amusements, to say nothing of the bad example. . . . The modern dance ought not to be tolerated in any decent society.[36]

The announcement that a certain minister was having a classic dancer to lecture in his church on "The Moralizing Effect of Dancing on the Human Soul," extends "beyond the wildest flights of our imagination."[37]

> What fools some preachers make of themselves! They shame the face of God. They delight the heart of the devil. All the little demons laugh at their blindness, while all the imps that kindle the eternal fire snicker at their insipidity.[38]

Indeed, the whole situation is a most serious one. The Methodists, like their Lutheran contemporaries, urge "the co-operation of the home, the school, and the Church"[39] in dealing with the matter.

The American Hebrew, with its "liberal" banner flying, will agree no jot or tittle with Methodism's advocating the curtailing of dancing. Every one will readily admit that some of the extreme dances need correction. "But the Methodist outcry against all dancing is a part of the Puritan revival which seeks to take the joy out of life."[40]

The Baptists speak out rather forcefully in their three official organs, *The Baptist, The Word and Way*, and *The Watchman-Examiner*, and, regardless of shadings of opinion that might be discernible in some instances, on the question of dancing, there is a striking similarity of attitude.

Members of the Southern Convention speaking through *The Word and Way* are convinced that there is nothing good that anyone can truthfully say of the dance.

> [Its] history furnishes abundant proof that its tendency is to demoralize. No one is ever helped by it either physically, intellectually, morally, or spiritually, while multitudes have been harmed and other multitudes wrecked and ruined. The dance is carnal exercise pure and simple. . . . The desire to dance is essentially carnal. The appealing thing to the dancer . . . is the sex impulse.[41]

The group would remind Christians that they are enjoined to "abstain from every appearance of evil,"[42] hence, such a thing as a dancing Christian must be written down as an "enemy of the Cross of Christ."[43] Beyond question "a dancing church member is a misnomer and everywhere and always a church and Christian liability."[44]

Feeling as the Baptists do about Christians who dance, it is understandable why a rumor that at least 95 per cent of their churches "were winking at dancing and tolerating it upon the part of their members"[45]—and even on Sunday evenings—galvanized the group into making a request asking for answers from at least one thousand pastors as to the truth or falsity of the rumor.[46]

> It is hard to believe that there is in our very midst, and at our very doors such spiritual apostasy, such prostitution of the Christian religion, and such scandalizing of an institution itself a Church of Christ. What a miserable caricature of our holy religion! How traitorous to Christ and to His cause. How utterly alien to Christ's spirit, and how

utterly subversive of His program. It is virtually a repudiation of everything essentially Christian.[47]

The kind of influence exerted by a church encouraging dancing is calculated to do young people vastly more harm than help. It were better far that young people be not brought under the influence of such a church. And reasons are obvious:

> It lowers the Christian standard of living to zero. It encourages the young people in the gratification of their carnal desires and leads them to believe that they can serve the devil to the very limit if only their performances have over them the thin disguise of a Christian profession . . . [and] a church and a pastor committed to the false and corrupting influence of modernism.[48]

From letters coming to the editor's desk relative to the above request, the journal informs its readers it is sorry to learn that, while dancing is not approved by any of their churches, many of them tolerate it on the part of some members. In rare cases, if at all, do the churches think of disciplining their members for the breach.

> This is all very regrettable. It means on the part of our church an inexcusable and lamentable tolerance of worldliness. It means the lowering of the Christian standard and an impoverishing of spiritual life. It means a hurtful and lamentable concession to the world.[49]

Baptists of the Northern Convention, while not quite as vocal as their southern neighbors, feel they have authority on their side when they do speak. Miss Irene Castle, "one of the leaders of the day in all manner of aesthetic modern dancing,"[50] is presented to speak in their stead:

> I'm horrified at the manner of dancing. . . . It is simply unspeakable. It is a shame and a disgrace that police have to be retained by hotels to supervise dancing, yet that is what is being done nightly in New York.[51]

If young people think of ministers of the church as "old-fogeyish," Baptists hope that the words of Miss Castle will convince them about certain phases of dancing.[52]

Relative to a problem similar to the type that harried the editors of *The Word and Way*, namely, dancing in lecture rooms, church parlors, and parish houses, *The Watchman-Examiner* admits it is old-fashioned enough to ask, "What would Christ think about such things if he were here on earth?"[53] In effect, the question is merely a rhetorical one, for "it is inconceivable that Christ would approve of the whirl of the modern dance in a building dedicated to his glory, or that he would approve of his church authorizing or superintending such affairs."[54] In general, the organ believes that some churches, in their effort to give their young people "a good time,"[55] are overdoing the entertainment business to the neglect of their primary mission.

The same journal is anxious to pass on to its readers what it considers to be an apt definition of jazz. The word has been in common use for some time, yet there are "some benighted souls who to this day do not know what is meant by the term."[56]

Jazz is ragtime plus blues, plus orchestral polyphony; it is the combination, in the popular music current, of melody, rhythm, harmony, and counterpoint.[57]

The periodical "now that attention has been called to it" decides "jazz does sound something like that—only where do 'melody' and 'harmony' come in?"[58]

The Unitarians are somewhat piqued by what they term "sidestepping." Their protest comes over the problem of dancing in church buildings. That problem, as has been seen, was causing quite a furor in some denominations. The section questions the logic of those who say, to tolerate church members who dance is one thing; for the church to sponsor dances, is quite another. If dancing is good, it is good; if it is not good, it is not good sometime. It is time the churches take a stand for one or the other.[59]

What the Presbyterians long wished to say about jazz, but refrained on grounds of modesty, they now feel they may say with impunity since an English music critic has expressed himself in a similar vein. This particular expert states that "the typical jazz composer or jazz enthusiast is an instrumental illiterate who is absurdly pleased with little things because he does not know how little they are."[60] With some naivete the group realizes why it revolted when jazz was imposed on the country: the Presbyterians did not have the "proper degree of brainlessness to appreciate this relic of the tom-toms of savagery."[61]

"Remembering that our Blessed Lord uses 'music and dancing' as symbolic of the joys of Heaven over a sinner's return,"[62] the Episcopalians will have none of the precisionist's displeasure at the thought of rhythmic motion. But surely the ugly, tuneless, vulgar savagery of jazz dancing has nothing in common with celestial melodies.

The debased imagination of its "composers" has evidently taken the highly accentuated "music" of tom-toms and hollow drums in the African jungle, to which naked cannibals are wont to prance, multiplied it according to some mechanical rule which has neither imagination nor inspiration, and set it forth to degrade the ears and feet of American youth.[63]

The contemporary Methodist publication does not conceal its satisfaction nor withhold its benediction in regard to the Episcopalian drive against jazz music and jazz dancing. "In view of the fact that Episcopalian leaders have always been regarded as being rather lax toward worldly amusements,"[64] this sounds rather strange coming from them. "There must be great danger in these jazz practices if the Episcopalians are so aroused. And we think they are not needlessly aroused."[65]

Cela saute aux yeux that the stately waltzes and decorous polkas of the older generation were but cherished memories in the decade of the 1920's. And those who followed the dictum that it mattered not who wrote the laws of the land as long as worthy sons wrote its songs, felt strangely out of place where new popular songs experienced an accelerated ephemeralness.

Perhaps the cry from the long-buried past had been slightly modified. "People no longer care to be mourned to, that they may weep for their sins, but to be piped to, that they may dance."[66]

"Our earth is degenerate in these latter days. There are signs that the world is speedily coming to an end. Children no longer obey their parents."

Translation of an ancient
Assyrian tablet, 2800 B. C.

CHAPTER VII

Fashions and Fads

Every age of history has witnessed the law of change at work in institutions, attitudes, and trends new and peculiar to the time. But, perhaps, few, if any, eras displayed the insatiable zest for what was new and untried that the decade of the 1920's evinced. And nowhere were more apparent the innovations that rushed to take advantage of the welcome than in the realm of what might be termed "fashions and fads."

With unwonted energy, the young generation set into motion a revolution bringing in its wake violent changes as to what youth did and how youth dressed. This sartorial revolution in its various phases was distressingly alarming to the traditional-minded; and public opinion became peevish and began to assert itself as antipathetic in most cases.

We shall first consider the aspect of fashions. Feminine apparel knew fluctuation before the 1920's, to be sure. However, it seems evident that the styles had always changed gradually, and hence, not shockingly: they, like the British constitution, simply "evolved."[1] Perhaps, it was more the quickness and unanimity with which changes were accomplished than the changes themselves, which startled alike parents, teachers, moral preceptors, and editors of religious periodicals. On the whole, however, in the realm of fashions, tones mollified and at times conciliatory, are employed.

Writing in the first year of the decade, *The Lutheran* first establishes its right to speak:

If a court judge pauses long enough in a court trial to moralize on the question of the proper attire of a woman witness, and if the authorities of our seashore resorts appoint female officers to see to it that women along the beach are properly clothed, the preacher can be pardoned if, now and then, he raises his voice in protest of prevailing fashions in women's clothes. And what he says on the question is by no means to be ridiculed. In fact, he is but voicing the sentiments of a vast number of people to whom the present fashion vogue is nauseating, and who applaud any preachment . . . on his part in the matter.[2]

The group places itself to a man behind a priest in New Orleans, who, according to report, refused to perform a wedding ceremony until the bride was garbed modestly.[3]

Those who insist that such scrupulosity is no longer in keeping with the temper of the times, that matters of social convention constantly change, are reminded that there is never an excuse for immodesty. Nor is this the opinion only of the "prudish"; those who consider themselves "liberal and progressive" have been "dumbfounded and hurt over the recent conduct of young girls in relation to their clothes."[4] The dress, or rather the lack of dress, of American women, has even become the subject for jest in the daily press, and it grieves this group of Lutherans to see women cheapened by their dress.

In individual cases it is perhaps difficult to decide how much of our modern female fashion is to be attributed to weakness of mind and how much to weakness of character. . . . The world jests and laughs at these things, but the poor creatures at whose expense it laughs are paying an awful price to provide this merriment.[5]

The situation is of such a nature as to attract even the state legislatures. This, the journal sees as a presage of what might prove to be a solution: perhaps laws against immodest dress will be forthcoming. The organ of Lutheran thought cites the instance of a bill pending in Utah providing "fine and imprisonment for those who wear on the street skirts higher than three inches above the ankle,"[6] and notes that similar bills limiting the length and depth of skirts and "decolletees" have been drawn up in other States.[7] However, there is too much evidence of a general lack of interest, the periodical fears, but it would remind the apathetic public that the matter is serious. "Immodesty and its consequences are the cause of the eternal damnation of multitudes."[8]

"How many strange fashions come and go,"[9] muses the Episcopalian group. Opinion here seems to carry with it an impassive and imperturbable attitude compared with the disquietude discernible among the Lutherans. Various quirks, rather than styles as such, gaining prominence, are assailed in comments strangely compounded of amusement and vexation.

One absurd custom which occurs to the editor is "the painful method whereby some women hold their coats together by their left hand, having cut away the button which would save them the trouble. The effect is as if each person were suffering from acute appendicitis."[10]

And "another imbecility which is evidently contagious,"[11] is brought to the reader's attention: namely, the wearing of an overcoat with the collar half turned-up. Were it done for need of protection against cold, the habit might have some foundation in reason. But as it is at the time, "it is difficult to imagine an absurdity greater than deliberately to affect that dégagé fashion."[12] A look at the men in the street will convince the dubious as to how widespread this idiotic custom has become.[13]

The passing of the "smooth-browed youth of our time" likewise elicits some signs of concern from the same religious group. The prevalence of a fashion for going bareheaded in all sorts of weather is to be deplored for its folly. "From squinting into the bright sunshine,"[14] foreheads are wrinkling into painful knots.

Those wrinkles tend to become permanent, so that what ought to be a painful symptom of advancing years is a premature possession of immaturity. . . . "Lifting the face" will be a poor remedy.[15]

A fashion note in a recent issue of *Vogue* exasperated the editor of *The Living Church* and prompted him to quote for the "readers' edification." "Do wear pyjamas, if your figure and the type of people you are with permit, in place of a tea-gown and for informal dinners."[16] Absurdities, truly, never know their limits.

The launching of a campaign against immodest dress by a group within the Catholic Church causes this group of Episcopalians to speculate as to what its outcome will be.[17] By and large, the segment feels that custom, rather than absolute principle, should decide what is or is not modest. Furthermore, it is of the opinion that present-day fashions, generally speaking, "are in so many ways more sensible and seemly than those which have become outmoded."[18]

"We have not thought it worth while," rejoins the Methodists of the Southern division in the editorial columns of their official publication, "to say much about women and the way they dress."[19] The comparative silence, however, does not necessarily connote acquiescence, for "we do not think they always dress in a way that is best for their health or best for their morals and the morals of the opposite sex."[20] Rather, the truth is that criticisms offered by editors, ministers, and others do not seem to accomplish much by influencing women in their styles. Nevertheless, the group does not think a few remarks to be ill-timed at this point. It is eager to commend the announcement of the Clothing Manufacturers that skirts having reached "a precarious height" are to lengthen again. "The knee length may be popular in Paris, but . . . the . . . short skirt apparently has no friends in this country."[21] However hopeful future practice may be, the group is nonetheless harassed by the fact that at the moment styles prevalent even among high school girls are endangering the morals of the boys. "Short skirts, silk and open work hose, low cut waists, and other outrages"[22] are making the dress of the adolescent "much worse than ever before."[23]

Paging through other contemporary Methodist publications, the group culls some observations and statements which might profitably be passed on to a wider circle. In the matter of bathing attire, for instance, there is an inevitable undermining of modesty.

> The fact that this modern scanty attire is so general and so popular in no sense indicates that it is either sensible or morally safe. How is it possible for a young woman to expose her person deliberately before the eyes of men and not lose that keen sense of modesty that was one of the ornaments of our mothers?[24]

Clothes affect one's personality, and in the midst of the drift toward social indecency through which the age is passing, the Christian conscience must be sufficiently vigorous to withstand the current.[25] It is well to remember that "the old kiss-me-quick bonnets of 1870 have been superseded by styles just as misleading."[26] If motives other than Christian decency be asked as regards the type of shoes prevalently worn, the health of womanhood should be incentive enough to bring concerted demand for lowering heels.[27]

In accents closely akin in tone to the Methodist voice, the group of Northern Baptists concede that they, too, have maintained a degree of reticence in regard to fashion, for "we do not profess to be an authority on styles, especially those of women."[28] But the group cannot but express amazement at the ease with which the extremes in garb are adopted. And since this is the fact, were styles determined by the better element in the community, many problems of present-day fashions would be minimized or even eliminated.

Certain references which found their way from editorial desks of various denominations into official periodicals give evidence, though indirectly, that Catholic sentiment was likewise aroused. We learn from such a source that a crusade was led, by the Third Order of Saint Francis in 1920, urging such things as the elimination of low-necked gowns, short sleeves, tight skirts, and transparent hose.[29] The Methodist journal notes that the Archbishop of Milwaukee issued orders to the effect that the priests of his diocese should make intensive efforts to supplant the disgusting shamelessness of the scandalous fashions with maidenly modesty.[30]

In 1927, the Baptists comment on a recent address of Pope Pius XI in which he denounced the present tendency in fashions, calling on "all who still have a sense of human nobility and dignity . . . to find a means of creating dams against a current so ugly and so ruinous and carrying so many catastrophes with it."[31] The Methodist journal makes reference to the same address of the Holy Father, and is of a mind that "the future will doubtless see changes in dress, perhaps additions, since women have now about reached the limit in discarding unnecessary clothing."[32]

Another phase of this revolution in fashions and fads—one which was even more disturbing to the older generation than changes in style of dress—was the freer use of cosmetics. Like the other changes in fashion, the cosmetic urge was democratic in that it knew no class barrier. Manufacturers of cosmetics saw their business increase eight-fold within the span of one decade from 1914-1925.[33]

Statistics, it has often been remarked, can prove anything that a skilled manipulator wants them to prove. On the other hand, there is a sheer force in figures, and the estimates of French perfumers that seventy-one per cent of the women of the United States use perfumes; ninety-five per cent, face powder; seventy-three per cent, toilet water; fifty-five per cent, rouge, seem fairly significant.[34]

Conceding that the word "cosmetician" may be new, the Presbyterians ingeniously recall that the business is very, very old. "Some of the contents of Tutankhamen's tomb were rare and costly cosmetics which, it was supposed, he would need to maintain his royal beauty unspoiled by the hand of death."[35] But it was not until the present time that the business has become a profession, with Americans expending more than two billion dollars a year to maintain and enhance their beauty. Despite the seven thousand different kinds of

"paints, and rouges, and lipsticks, and ointments" the group ruefully admits

> it is pitiful to see the face painted and overlaid with all manner of
> these artificial enhancements that are not even skin deep and will
> wash off like whitewash, while the deeper face of the soul is un-
> adorned and marred with an unhappy disposition and evil spirit.[36]

The Lutherans are in the same school of thought as their Presbyterian contemporaries in this matter. "It is painful to see young girls
. . . paint and powder themselves and spoil their beauty."[37] This
group would have youth taught to realize that the greatest gift is
the charm and beauty of goodness. To ape the cosmetics of the
demimonde is to forget that "beauty unadorned is adored most."[38]

A bit more prosaic are the Baptists who tell us that as they
wander through the streets in "this day of cosmetics" they are reminded forcefully of the lovely Quaker woman who had a formula
for beauty all her own.

> I use for the lips, truth; for the voice, prayer; for the eyes, pity;
> for the hands, charity; for the figure, uprightness; and for the heart,
> love.[39]

Lamentations over the huge cost to the nation of "vanity cases"
do no good, in the estimation of the Unitarian group. Style, they
note, is a capricious thing, and the day will undoubtedly come when
women shall discover that the human face is more beautiful when
left as nature shaped it, even though she may not have been too kind
in her gift.[40]

The fact that the people of the United States spend more for
cosmetics than for education and religion combined, provides those
who have made a pastime of reviewing American culture an argument for leveling charges of materialism against the nation. "But,"
this religious denomination asks, "why not? What is the harm in
making a good deal of money, and enjoying the making and spending of it?"[41] Probably the excessive use of cosmetics lies in the fact
that ten wish to adorn the body where one is eager to get knowledge.

> We are physical beings, first, with clamorous appetites to satisfy,
> one of which is that of personal adornment. . . . Religion may insist
> that to develop the mind and beautify the soul is the chief end of all
> living; but all the same the costs of physical adornment will con-
> tinue to mount.[42]

In this whole matter, the group would advise toleration. "Let evolution do her perfect work; in the end it will, through spiritual culture, provide that nucleus about which will gather higher ideas of beautifying our physical selves."[43]

The Jewish segment would detain us but a moment with a remark laconic but well-calculated. It has to do with a phase of the upheaval in fashions and fads over which other denominations are apparently unconcerned: bobbed hair. "New excavations in Palestine substantiate the assertion . . . that in Israel of the Saul and David era women wore their hair bobbed."[44] The journal naively leaves to the reader the privilege of drawing conclusions, remarking but incidentally that "these ancient Israelites had wine presses also."[45]

During these years of change, the American girl made her way into the ranks of smokers. There could be no mistake that she had come. In the period 1911-1915 the number of cigarettes sold annually averaged less than fifteen billion; for the period 1921-1925 sales averaged well over sixty-five billion. During the same period there was no marked increase in the sale of cigars, and chewing tobacco fell off in receipts.[46] Hence, it would seem safe to conclude that the increased cigarette demand did not indicate a more intense tobacco hunger,—but, rather, new smokers. The religious press reserved its most thunderous declamations for this aspect of the "revolution."

Methodists of both Northern and Southern divisions erase whatever lines of demarcation might exist between them and practically unite on this issue with a condemnation that is unanimous and a plea that is earnest. To America's womanhood, the group counsels: "Crush the habit! Be merciless. Forget about clemency. And America's manhood will rise up and call you blessed."[47]

The advertisers are rapped vigorously for their part in the widespread cigarette habit among both sexes. Young men are beguiled through specious words.

> By the ingenious use of the names of famous athletes the advertisers would suggest to hero-worshipping youth that the way to obtain the strong limbs, stout hearts, steady nerves which they desire is to suck nicotine into the delicate apparatus which nature has provided for breathing fresh air.[48]

And the greed of the tobacco sellers leads them to use every seductive argument to deceive young women into believing that the use of the cigarette not only improves the health, but enhances the personal charm of the smoker. Actually, the facts are definitely contrariwise.

Apart from the dirt and foul odors which inevitably go along with the habit and which are so foreign to the ideal of womanly delicacy, there are practical considerations based upon the special function of the sex which, in the opinion of many of the best physicians, raise a serious question concerning the coming generation born of nicotine addicts.[49]

The group would arraign the advertisers not only for the bland assertions which sprawl across the pages of the newspapers, but also for the seductive sales arguments which are being forced into the family circle through the radio. Parents would becomingly bestir themselves to consider the baneful effects of cigarettes on immature physique and feminine nerves, and vocally resent "the intrusion of a loud speaker bawling out the false commendations of Luckies and Unluckies."[50]

The patience of those Methodists who devote themselves to the public welfare is taxed almost beyond limit by the insidious use that tobacco manufacturers are making of billboards in order to inveigle young women into smoking.

> Some time ago the young and beautiful woman appeared on the billboard as an interested spectator; gradually she increased her interest until now she is boldly pictured as enjoying a smoke.[51]

The psychology of the poster is evident to all, and if the manufacturers are permitted to continue their suggestive advertising, they will doubtless greatly increase their sales.

Feeling, perhaps, that there is strength in numbers, the editor, as is a rather frequent custom with the Methodist group, summons a fellow editor with whom he is in hearty agreement, and with undisguised confidence quotes:

> Women of judgment and sense . . . are all dead set against the tobacco habit. It will die after a brief vogue, with a few fools who, like moths, have not sense enough to keep from singeing themselves at the flame.[52]

With cool disdain, *The American Hebrew* scornfully derides "the Puritan Alexanders, who having banished the beer glass and the whiskey bottle, are longing for more worlds to conquer."[53] Their newest venture is an anti-tobacco crusade. After that, the Jewish segment hazards, in tones tinged with sarcasm, there will be anti-coffee and anti-tea campaigns, and still more and more triumphs to win.

With the ultimate abolition of Dancing, the Movies, the Theatre, and Baseball, we shall reach Nirvana. Maybe, however, we shall be permitted, if we do it very gently, to tweedle our thumbs.[54]

Remote and far removed from Jewish sentiment, the Presbyterian group, with ill-concealed irritability takes its position. An appalling thought, indeed, is it that the cigarette in its apparently innocent but treacherous form holds in its grip so large a number of youth. Its legacy to this choice portion of Americans is nothing more than "a lowered physical vitality, a beclouded mentality, and a weakened morality."[55] Opinion pens a panegyric:

The cigarette, what a camouflage! Short, but long enough to shorten life; mild, but strong enough to be a chain of bondage; weak, but dense enough to darken the whole sky line of youth's ambition and success.[56]

With sentiments that are similar, but in a mood more lithesome, the editor of another journal of the Presbyterian denomination parcels out some morsels of direction.

If we were proffering advice to a young man concerning the choosing of a wife, would we solemnly counsel him to select as his life partner one who habitually fills the circumambient atmosphere with ill-smelling exhalations? If we were confronted with the alternation of entering into wedlock with such a specimen of womanhood or of living an exile amid the tall timber, we would choose the latter without a moment's hesitation.[57]

Lutheran opinion, as seen in the pages of its official journal, appears somewhat mellow and inclined towards a limited toleration in this matter of fads and fashions. Only in the case of the cigarette does it take exception. "We have laboriously accustomed ourselves," the group avers, "to fashions that are very different from those in vogue in the days of our youth."[58]

Probably the majority of us "oldsters" are willing to accept the reasonableness of abbreviated dresses and amputated tresses as practical and in themselves proper. But the idea persists that the use of cigarettes by girls and women detracts from their charm.[59]

The habit-forming aspect of tobacco is in itself to be abhorred, but above and beyond that is the poisonous nature of nicotine. "No amount of good music and sky writing can extract the habit-forming, nerve-stimulating, digestive-disturbing effect of smoking."[60] The denomination predicts a wave of public sentiment being aroused to forbid smoking unless a conservative check is administered.[61]

Dipping into editorial columns of the official periodicals, one finds that sentiment among Baptists converges on two principal problems relative to smoking: college legislation and advertising tactics. Of the opinion that the smoking woman in college tends to give the cigarette the standing of a mark of culture, the group commends specifically and by name, several colleges for recent edicts against student-smoking.[62] Scant but highly unfavorable darts are aimed against those institutions reported to have sanctioned smoking on their campuses. "The modern college miss who smokes may seem chic and smart to herself," the editor solliloquizes, "but she loses that marvelous and charming grace—femininity."[63]

Stinging words are reserved for the advertisers. A display in a daily paper portraying a popular woman "telling with smiling face and enthusiasm of the solace, mental balm, and enjoyment she gets out of a certain brand of cigarettes,"[64] seems conclusively indicative that greed knows no limit but the opportunity for gain. One of the newer and equally despicable schemes of the "social anarchists" is advertising through the channel of the radio.[65] These advertisers of cigarettes may regretfully realize one of these days that they have overdone their business. From many quarters, this religious group affirms, have challenges come on the part of "medical men, school authorities, athletes, and others."[66] The tobacco business may be manufacturing "rope wherewith to hang itself."[67]

The laymen in the editorial office of *The Commonweal*, as well as the group of Catholics for whom they are vocal, would prefer fewer citations about and incitations against tobacco users.

> Were all the hard things that have been said about nicotine justified in medical fact, the citizenry of the Union, male and female, would by now be wards of the state, and only psychopaths would be free to make any decisions at all.[68]

Statisticians, too, the Catholics feel, are inducted into questionable service much too frequently. It is conceded, of course, that statistics are always fascinating, and even "the habit of thinking in billions which is one of the aftermaths of the war gives figures a breath-taking quality all their own."[69] But when the number of cigarettes allegedly sold soars to a height where only the processes of arithmetical progression can follow them, it may be that numbers, "by proving too much, prove nothing at all."[70]

Notwithstanding a tolerant attitude on smoking as such, the *America* does not approve of smoking by the fairer sex. The results of a religious and moral survey for the year 1924-1925 which was conducted at Notre Dame University give, the journal would have us believe, a peerless commentary on feminine perfection. Young men, in overwhelming numbers, preferred as prospective wives girls who do not smoke, drink, swear, or lie.

> If the modern girl's departure from so many ideals that have become sacred, has been calculated to further her prospects of winning admirers, her ambition, it would seem, is somewhat destined to fail. Young men may find the "flapper" type interesting, but their interest does not promise to endure.[71]

The *America* likewise informs us that it would question, with its contemporary, *The Commonweal,* "how well advised the manufacturers are in initiating campaigns to spread the habit of smoking among young girls."[72]

As for the moral side of the problem, the journal thinks the air has become heavy with muddled thinking. Concisely and clearly, it attempts clarification.

> Tobacco, like any other creature of God, is to be used or not used, in accord with the dictates of reason and conscience. To drink tobacco, as our ancestors would have it, or to dine on a beef-steak is in itself an indifferent act.[73]

Just as one may call for beef to quicken one's failing energies, or to display contempt for the law of abstinence, so too, a variety of motives may induce one to smoke.[74]

Somewhat impatiently would this group of Catholics take issue with the statements relative to fatal effects with which the unborn generation will be visited because of smoking mothers. No proof exists, the section holds, for the unmodified assertion that tobacco is a baby killer. Fanaticism lies at the very heart of much of the current crusading, and wisely may all be wary lest the head succumb to the heart. The cigarette is here to stay and its widespread acceptance has robbed it of much of its former opprobrium.

Two generations ago the stage villain always smoked a cigarette. It was the badge of his tribe, signifying that wickedness could not further go. Sunday schools and mothers warned their charges against it. Heavy-jowled olders whose recreation was a cigar as thick as a rope, jeered at it. But today the cigarette is as numerous as bootleggers. . . . Its manufacturers endow . . . colleges, and pay a high percentage of our income and corporation taxes.[75]

Indeed, the wheel has gone half turn. "Nowadays even a clergyman can smoke a cigarette without subjecting his orthodoxy or his moral rectitude to suspicion!"[76]

With an asperity usually uncommon to its group opinion, the Unitarians intimate that their attitude in this problem is on the side of the reformers. The number of people who use tobacco is highly significant as to the grip the weed has on the nation, and the social problem that smoking posits, compels attention and demands solution.[77]

The methods employed by advertisers concern the Unitarians just as they called forth comment from several of the denominations considered above. Righteously, *The Christian Register* contends, do the reformers claim that tobacco interests are deceiving and ruining the health of multitudes. Advertisers may assure the unsuspecting that "there is not a cough in a carload," or that "reaching for a Lucky instead of a sweet,"[78] spells health. The unyielding truth is that "the excessive use of cigarettes . . . dwarfs growing bodies, promotes intestinal catarrh, palpitation of the heart, anaemia, cancer of the mouth, loss of teeth, premature age. . . ."[79] Regardless of what its personal opinion is, however, the group does not wish to appear querulous and is careful to insist that "we are not arguing about it— we are just telling the world."[80] Neither "are we denying the right of anyone to enjoy the consolations of smoking."[81]

Should women smoke? The Unitarians admit that among women who do smoke, some ladies may be found. "But it was not so among the first women in our own day who smoked. They were distinctly of the demimondes."[82] A habit which man may practice with some degree of impunity is not suitable for women since it robs them of their chief charm.

The younger set of the 1920's which shortened its skirt, bobbed its hair, and smoked its cigarette was perhaps no richer in money or poorer in soul than the many generations which had trod this earth before it. To what extent the shifting manners in fashions penetrated the bedrock of moral character is academic speculation. Perhaps one of the definitions of jazz—"brazen defiance of accepted rules,"—might serve equally well to describe the spirit of much of the generation.

"The stage but echoes back the
                    public voice."

—Samuel Johnson, *Prologue at the
Opening of the Drury Lane Theatre.*
I, 52.

CHAPTER VIII

The Cinema Craze

Forgetting the past and the future in order to taste to the full the delights of the present, the flamboyant spirit of the 1920's did whatever it put its hand or heart to, in the superlative. *Virtus stat in medio* was for the generation a dictum quite as dead as the Roman scribe whose quill first traced the words. Proudly and boastfully, it counted its millions and billions of everything: money, automobiles, grandstand spectators, cigarettes,—and movie-goers.

It was during this period that the motion picture became one of the most popular pastimes in all parts of the country, and one of the weekly habits of a large portion of the population. The movie industry had come a long way from its humble beginnings back in the "gay '90's," when, through the experiments of Thomas Edison, crude machines capable of throwing animated pictures on a screen were developed. Passing through days of the penny arcade, and later of the so-called "nickelodeons," the motion picture, about 1915, began to capture the popular fancy. The business had an astonishing growth, and, with increasingly better films, the public began flocking to performances. By the middle of the 1920's it moved into position of fourth largest industry in the country, representing a capital investment of more than one and a half billion dollars, and drawing a weekly attendance at theaters estimated at the phenomenal figure of 100,000,000.

Sensuous and sensational themes so frequently featured in the new films brought a rising storm of continual and caustic criticism from church organizations. Placatingly, the motion-picture producers, early in the decade, installed Will H. Hays, President Harding's Postmaster General, as their arbiter of morals and of taste. Efforts and endeavors actually accomplished little more than devising a system of paying lip service to the old code of morals while offering incense to the new. And throughout most of the decade, threats of censorship alternated with promulgations of a new series of moral commandments for the producers to follow.

Meanwhile, printers' ink was flowing in profusion.

"What further need have we of witnesses?"[1] ask the Lutherans of the Missouri Synod with their mind's eye on the objectionable and immoral pictures. "Hearken to the world confessing to its own shame that 'men love darkness rather than light. . . .' "[2] The producers insist that inoffensive, decent shows are not patronized: "bad" pictures are good investments, while "good" pictures are losing propositions. "The movie men are right—men love filth rather than purity. . . . Men are much more willing to bring sacrifices to an idol than to accept blessings from the true God."[3]

Writing in 1920, the United Lutherans, chagrined and disillusioned at the rupture of what multitudes had considered a charming "star" marriage, consider that Mary Pickford and Douglas Fairbanks have struck a flagrant blow at the sacredness of wedlock.[4] Much that these two actors have done for picture land has been unobjectionable, but now "they have put on the screen of real life a divorce picture at which no Christian can look without deep pain and disgust."[5]

Like their fellow Lutherans, this group is greatly concerned at the disregard of modesty and decency on the part of both the producer and the public in those moving pictures which are advertised as the best. "The lengths to which the industry, for filthy lucre's sake, has gone to please the vulgar tastes of a susceptible public is astounding."[6]

With some degree of satisfaction, this denominational segment, by the late summer of 1924, is able to note that the long and loud protests—though by no means as many or as vigorous as were called for—seem to be having their effect. "The terrible sex slush that was much in evidence several years ago, the subtle and often brazen immoral suggestiveness of many plays, have not appeared in any of the pictures we have seen this year."[7] However, popular clamor for what is comic has induced the industry to provide pictures of that type very liberally, and unfortunately some of these are much overdone and have become ludicrous in an attempt to cater to the tastes of the groundlings. When this tendency to exaggeration and distortion is halted, it is hoped that motion pictures will cease to be a menace to the morals of people, both young and old.[8]

It would seem that Methodists of the Southern Conference did not attend the same theaters that the Lutherans patronized in 1924. For, in this year, speaking through the editorial column of their paper, the Methodists are of the opinion that if Mr. Will Hays, "motion picture dictator since 1922,"[9] has accomplished anything towards making moving pictures cleaner, it is difficult to see improvement. "Too many heavy investors in the business are men of no very high moral ideas. The vast business is greatly influenced by the motive of profit, whatever be the effect on the community."[10] But the stark truth is that picture shows are in our midst and are likely to stay. With their daily attendance as great as the enrollment in the public schools of the country, their influence is beyond words to describe.[11] The group further feels that censorship can do something but that patrons can do even more in correcting the evils of the reels. Proprietors are sensitive to the tastes of their patrons. In most American communities there are enough high-minded citizens to guarantee prosperity to a picture house properly managed. "Overcome evil with good"[12] must be the rule for the Christian.

The editor of *The Christian Advocate* judiciously reflects on some of the statements of his co-workers in the field of religious journalism. He is in sympathetic alarm with another Methodist editor who sees that "serious crimes, including even murder, have been traced directly to the moving picture theater."[13] His wrath is aroused with still another editor, who uncovers the tactics of moving picture operators to desecrate the Sunday in the name and under the guise of charitable purposes.

> Shows are running on Sunday with the proceeds of the initial presentation going to charity. Charity not only covers a multitude of sins, but it serves to bring a few of them to light. . . . The collection plate may be passed once, but when they have won their point—never again.[14]

In concurrence with a secular correspondent, the Methodist editor gives some deliberation on evil results often overlooked: the fomenting of national envy and class jealousy. The unbounded wealth that is presented on the screen is not conducive to happy and satisfied contentment.

> Everyone in the movies can afford a telephone. At the disposal of every one . . . is an expensive automobile. The movie Cinderella may commence her career in some small town, but it is only to continue

it in mansions which, by their number, variety, and size, would tax the modest purse of a Vanderbilt or a Morgan. A dinner party is set in a style that impels one to regret the simplicities of Louis XIV. And the costumes,—well, even an average dancer is as extravagantly gowned as a drawing room at Buckingham Palace.[15]

This impression of a lavish luxury unparalleled in the history of civilization is not true of the majority of individual Americans, although collectively we may be a rich people. Comparatively few of the people "enter the charmed circle that has time and money to pose on the terrace in the moonlight."[16]

The Northern Conference evinces a measure of resentment against the movies on the charge that the industry "wants to make money seven days a week."[17] The producers, the group would have its contemporaries know, are making a concerted effort "to persuade the gullible public that some monstrous Blue Law Reformer is demanding ironclad legislation that will make it a crime to go anywhere on Sunday except to church."[18] However, there is a deep assurance, judging from the past, that all attempts to desecrate the Sunday will ultimately come to naught. "This is the way the recently liquidated firm of John Barleycorn and Company used to use the papers to fight its battles. But it lost. And the moving picture men will lose, too . . . for they are wrong, and the wrong cannot finally win."[19]

This section's sense of decency is outraged. The salacious and criminal scenes in a great number of films are on the increase. But even were these eliminated, there would still be work for the censor who would conscientiously strive to make the picture helpful rather than hurtful. Several fields lie open for this improvement: caricaturing and comedy. "The habit of caricaturing the clergymen—always excepting the Catholic priest—is atrociously prominent. It ought to be cut out—which is technical and not slang in film circles."[20] Then the kind of comedy often used to enliven an otherwise heavy program—"the slap-stick and horse-play" type—is nothing but an abomination to spectators having "both taste and sense."[21] For the satisfaction of the curiosity of one who might be puzzled as to reasons for the popularity of moving pictures, this group has the answer as psychologists would have it. "No degree of intelligence is needed. No attitude toward anything and no conviction on anything is necessary. The fascination lies in not knowing what one will see."[22] This is not especially complimentary to the people who pride themselves on being intelligent, who know at least one language, who have convictions, and who ought to be immune to the titillation of the unexpected.[23]

Equally indignant over the matter of Sunday movies are Baptist neighbors in the North. Scathing words uttered in a perturbed air are voiced against those who have recently led a bitter attack on the men and women who believe that Sunday should not be given over to commercialism. In cartoon, in picture, and in print, these Christians have been maligned, presented as bigots and joy killers, with purposes attributed to them of which they never dreamed. The group becomes more irate as it realizes that the natural result of such campaigning has been confusion and chagrin among well-meaning people.[24] These Northern Baptists, like Northern Methodists, are inclined to tender to the producers remembrances of how such methods have reacted previously. "A part of the American people can be fooled for a time but all American people return to sanity after a time."[25] The pictures themselves, are, in far too many instances, nothing more than a travesty of some of the most sacred relations of life.[26]

Judges of the country are finding evidence of causal connections between movies and crime and "these men are not talking theory. They have been giving the hard, cold facts of their experience on the bench, with concrete instances of the evils of which they speak."[27] And the moral outrage goes still further. "There are sex pictures, which for their power in forcing early development of the sexual instinct and for destroying the virginal purity of the mind, may be worse . . . than the pictures of crime."[28]

As long as box office receipts continue to be the guiding star of the motion-picture industry, so long will the finer qualities of human nature be sinned against. Promoters of movies are going as far as public sentiment will allow them. Isn't it time to clean the Augean stables?[29] Censorship is one step in the right direction.[30]

In terms more strident than those of the Northern Convention, the Southern Baptists express their opinion on Sunday movies. If the present trend continues uninterruptedly, the narrow margin between Sabbath observance and Sabbath desecration will be wiped out entirely. The group would remind everyone that the Sabbath is of divine institution, God-given, God-imposed, and laden with a divine sanction.[31]

Neither the individual nor the community nor the organization nor the nation can disobey the Sabbath law with impunity. Somehow, some way, some day the penalty must be paid. If this be true, and there can be no doubt about it, our nation is storing up judgment against the day of judgment. It is mortgaging its future. It is courting disaster.[32]

The Baptists behind *The Watchman-Examiner* are in absolute agreement. "We think Sunday movies are a disgrace. No Christian should under any circumstances buy a ticket and enter a Sunday movie."[33]

A needful admonition to pastors must be given at this point. "A moving picture theater at any time is no place for a minister of the gospel."[34]

A "moral" or "religious" show comes to town. The theater managers immediately send complimentary tickets to "the clergy" and many of them rise to the bait like a mountain trout and give to the manager a "noble" testimonial as to "the religious value" of the show in exchange for three-dollars worth of tickets.[35]

Religious shows are produced not with high moral purposes, but "to hoodwink" the public and even to form from the ranks of religious people new theater-goers. "The plan works like a charm, for going first to see 'religious' plays they soon get the theater habit, and when the theater habit becomes confirmed the prayer meeting habit loses its grip."[36]
A bellicose mood which cannot be gainsaid underlies the vituperative remarks which these Baptists aim at the producers of salacious and demoralizing pictures. These individuals, badly frightened by the movement toward censorship, are ready "to promise to be good, and never, never to be naughty again, or to allow naughty things to be seen on their screens."[37] But they are not to be trusted. When the scare is over, they will be back at their old tricks again.

When the devil was sick, the devil a saint would be;
When the devil was well, the devil of a saint was he![38]

This segment of Baptists would agree with Methodists that careful supervision and sharp censorship of every film is necessary but an aroused public sentiment is even more necessary. The operators realize that their most reliable and satisfactory patrons are the best people of the community, and not the "hoodlum" element; but, reckoning on past experience, the men in the business know that the decent-minded folk, however much they grumble, usually do nothing to give effect to their grumbling. The reasoning seems well-grounded.[39]

We criticize and complain—to ourselves—because of the scandalous nature of the picture we see tonight, then we go back to the same place tomorrow night to see what will be thrown on the screen then. The manager or producer chuckles and rubs his hands in glee. He is satisfying the baser element of his constituency; the better element, while not satisfied, is standing for it; and he is raking in the shekels from both classes.[40]

It is time for the upright to speak in no uncertain terms.

The eager spontaneity and evident determination with which all the religious denominational groups examined in this study hasten their pens along the page of journalism relative to the matter of the movies is indicative of the role the motion picture occupied in the thinking of the generation of the period. Heretofore, all groups have spoken on practically all aspects of society's manners, but seldom have they all spoken in each and every journal used in the present instance. Their ink varied in shade, it is true; sometimes black, sometimes white, and sometimes in different hues of grey,—but pens have rushed along putting thoughts into print with an impatient haste to have "their say."

And so we turn to the two Presbyterian journals and find that the publication, *The Presbyterian Banner*, supposedly representing the less-conservative school of thought is conceding "that the motion-picture business as it is now carried on, is about as demoralizing as the old-time drinking saloons and disreputable houses."[41] The other periodical takes offense at "the tendency in many motion-picture films to treat religious observances, particularly the marriage cere-mony, in a flippant way, making it the occasion for cheap comedy. . . ."[42] In view of the fact that the moving picture is a powerful avenue of approach to and entrance into the mind and the heart of all who look upon the animated screen, the perils and problems it raises are of portentous importance, and, as yet, censorship is not meeting the peril effectively.[43]

The Episcopalians are somewhat disputatious and in tones in-transigent condemn the "drinking and debauchery and crime and divorce and illicit love and jibes at religion and temperance and about everything worth while"[44] which are the stock-in-trade of most films.

Along with the Baptists this segment is prone to censure without pity the producers who make empty promises of reform.

> Regardless of what they promise, the business will not and cannot be cleaned up by the present movie industry, because so many of the men do not know what is clean. Their ideas of good and bad have reference only to the dollar. . . . To those who live all their lives in mud, mud is clean.[45]

To add to their concern is the undeniable fact that the Church is being outstripped by the movies in the race for influence upon the morals of the rising generation: very few children attend more than one Sunday school, and very many children go to the movies several times a week.[46] "The sooner we realize the filthiness of the cinema, and its tremendous influence upon the morals of the children, indeed upon the morals of the people generally, the better it will be for America."[47]

Sparks begin to fly when *The American Hebrew* gets into this discussion. The editor cannot contain his and his constituents' irritability, and fairly unrolls reels of trenchant criticism on "this state of affairs that is heading us toward restrictive censorship."[48] The coming of a censor, whether honest or hypocritical, is bound to be a blow to art, which cannot thrive in anything but free air. The real censors should be the public. Laws will never make up for the lack of basic decency and good taste. "It cannot be that only the morons and the half-wits rush to buy tickets for the obviously salacious concoctions."[49] In unmistakable terms, the Jewish segment reiterates its policy:

> *The American Hebrew* stands for decent pictures. It stands unalterably opposed to lewd, corrupting exhibitions. It maintains that the full penalty of the law should be visited on the guilty. No new machinery for enforcement, however, is necessary. . . . The present laws on the statute books of every State are amply sufficient to punish any person who either makes, distributes, or shows lewd and immoral pictures.[50]

The group raises its voice still more pronouncedly, and notes that from time immemorial censorships have been either stupid or corrupt or both. Water cannot rise higher than its level. A liberal education, a sense of the artistic, and an appreciation of fitness are not attributes to be acquired overnight by censors. The group questions the type of men the organizations for censorship have on their staffs.

They complain at the conspicuous absence of writers, artists, musicians, and ethical leaders of the first rank.[51] Their motives, too, are subjected to imputation.

These self-appointed guardians are not disseminating the teachings of Jesus Christ, especially his basic doctrine of love of one's fellow men. They preach bigotry and intolerance. It is their kind which turns houses of divine worship into breeding places of hate. The motion-picture industry in control of such men would have the artistic value of the Little Rollo books and the soporific effects of the sermons they deliver and the tracts they write. . . . We favor reform and progress, but we are utterly opposed to . . . puritan hysteria.[52]

Realistically and practically, the spokesman for the Unitarians ponders the problems of the movies over which his contemporaries are nettled. Deliberately dispassionate and calm in the midst of their verbal frays, he reflects that motion pictures are here to stay and to grow. In influence on public thinking and morals they are coming close to rivaling the schools and the churches. "Either we must take the pictures into camp or be taken into camp."[53] What seems new and strange in one age is usually accepted by the next generation. "Music in the churches staggered our forefathers until they began to see the force of Wesley's protest against letting the devil have all the good tunes."[54] To this group, regulation is but one side of the problem—the negative one: suppression of bad pictures. There is an open field for constructive work on the other side—the positive one: encouragement of good pictures. The law can stop bad pictures, but it cannot consistently compel good ones.[55] Producers and public will have to abide by "motion-picture ethics." "We must have standards. They may not be the best. We may criticize them, and wish to remove the fetters. But the fact remains that most of us are lost without standards of some sort."[56] Herein lies the major difficulty as the Unitarian group sees it. "Blood-and-thunder scenes, perverted notions of sex, exaggerated and impossible episodes, false ideals and unnatural results, form an opinion of life that is unreal."[57] Not suppression, then, but encouragement by way of education and persuasion will go far toward raising movies to a constructive art and a powerful influence for right thinking and high living.[58]

In the matter of comment on the movies, there seems to be some indecision in Catholic opinion. Perhaps conflicting views struggling for recognition in the public mind have produced articulation that lacks the peremptory tone usually discernible in the expressions of this section. From one point of view, the charge is leveled that movies are capable of paralyzing the mental processes of our children. Many educators, in fact, are learning that a considerable portion of classroom difficulties is directly traceable to the malign influences of the sensational motion pictures.[59]

> The daily meal for the child's insatiable mind is made up of shootings, stabbings, infernal contrivances for human torturing which never existed, beings half-man and half-beast, plotting, scheming, intrigue, inanities, sensationalism, vulgarism.[60]

All taste for good reading among students is thus apt to be destroyed. The child cares only for the story, and, if he is able to read it in the form of an animated picture, the written book will be neglected. "At its best, the film cannot take the place of a careful literary study of good models, yet were it brought somewhat closer to the canons of art, its present destructive influence would be greatly lessened."[61]

Notwithstanding, a great dawn in the future may even await the movies—a dawn when the movies may become stepping stones to great literature. But to make them such, "there is much more need of the fundamentals of art than there is of boards of censorship."[62]

The remaining group of Catholics voicing its opinions in the columns of *The Commonweal* gives evidence that in its estimation Mr. Hays has done a commendable task. In this tenet these Catholics, of course, differ from the Methodists of the Southern Conference.

> . . . though motion pictures are still frequently a source of danger to the young and a spur to the passions of elder men and women, a reasoned consideration of what has been accomplished by the system of co-operative censorship established by Mr. Will Hays shows that the producers are normally ready to make changes suggested by those who review pictures in the interest of public ethics.[63]

There is a hint of an admission that further improvement can still be made through the same system, but autocratic control is not the answer to undesirable films.

Thus, it is seen, that the motion pictures, bidding fair in the 1920's to become America's leading amusement, were, in great part, the burden of public thinking as evidenced in editorial comment. Distortion of life in all its phases is the charge most often hurled against the movies. But whether they led the way for the general "let-down" for the generation, or merely mirrored life of the period, is a question that is an academic one, and its possible solution need not detain us here.

In 1928, an event occurred that was to give the industry an impetus unparalleled in its relatively short history: the talking picture came, producers saw possibilities, and in a year the conquest over the silent film was virtually complete. However, the curtain drops on our decade at this point; hence, we write our

FINIS.

"The contagion of crime is
like that of the plague."

—Napoleon Bonaparte,
Sayings of Napoleon.

CHAPTER IX

Flagrant Failings

In the ebb and flow of human life throughout the timeless years, waves of lawlessness have been no novelty. But their size and frequency are highly variable, as is the nature of events which sets them in motion. During the decade of the 1920's in mountainous heaps, a surging wave of unprecedented power and violence buffeted the very fabric of American life.

Occupied as so many of the people were with "tremendous trifles," the onrush of the angry waters, threatening to undermine national foundations, was simply ignored under pressure of competing interests. So engrossing was the complex life of business, and so exacting the obligations of the life of pleasure, that erstwhile levees of righteousness and dikes of integrity were often neglected. The flood of lawlessness may appear a far cry from the revolt of youth against custom and convention, but there were observers who felt it was but a different manifestation of the same underlying current.

This wave of crime that threatened to engulf America in the Twenties had repercussions on practically all levels of life, and its frothy billows took various forms. However, in the present instance, our interest is confined to the expressions of public opinion on matters relative to society as such. For the sake of brevity, which is obviously necessary, limitations must be set up. Accordingly, three manifestations of lawlessness, apparently the most menacing ones to editors of religious journals, will receive the burden of our attention. They are crime as such, drug addiction, and student suicides; these will be considered in the order listed.

"Do you know," *The Presbyterian Magazine* asks in shocked alarm, "that America is the most lawless country in the world?"[1] In an earnest effort to arouse national pride, it resorts to comparison.

More robberies are committed in a year in Chicago than in all England, Scotland, and Wales. And on the basis of each 100,000 population, homicides were seven times as numerous last year in the United States as they were in Spain. The most disconcerting aspect behind these facts is that the majority of the crimes is committed by boys—the average hardened criminal being about seventeen years old.[2] Vice and crime are social enemies—symptoms of moral laxness and moral illiteracy.[3]

The tone of the more "liberal" wing of the Presbyterian group is not one of high-strung anxiety. There is not necessarily an absolute increase in the amount of crime; rather, a change in its character.

> The increase in crime . . . does not necessarily mean that there are more persons among us criminally inclined, for the vicious classes are always with us. More likely it is explained by . . . the better chances of escaping detection and conviction.[4]

Alerted also to the sorry fact that in a recent year more money was stolen in robberies than is required to run the government, the United Lutherans, with bated breath, tell the rest of the nation that reasons for this appalling epidemic of crime are not difficult to uncover:[5]

> First, the tremendous increase of luxurious living among the people taken as a whole; Second, the failure to punish crimes with swift and sure penalties; Third, the weakening of religious and moral restraints.[6]

When one considers that "fully seventy-five per cent of the filching has been done by youths under twenty-five years of age, many of them in their teens,"[7] the import of the serious collapse of the moral sense cannot be missed.

There can be no side-stepping, the Baptists would also admit with a sense of injured national pride. The United States must plead guilty to the indictment cited against it by the global family, namely, that America is the most lawless nation in the world.[8]

Probably American justice is not as prompt, adequate, and final as it should be.

> Whatever the causes of our high eminence in crime, our rapidly increasing lawlessness ought to be a matter of grave concern to every one who bears the name of American, and certainly to every Christian American.[9]

The editor of the official organ of Northern Baptists would hasten to include another possible reason to the three causes proposed above by the Lutherans.

The featuring of crime by newspapers makes the criminal seem a hero to those of his own class. Would not crime waves attain less proportions if attended by less publicity?[10]

The Catholics for whom the *America* speaks are convinced that religion and fixed principles of morality, based upon a definite religion, must rule the lives of people.[11] This group, too, sees causes contributing to placing America in her present unenviable position of leader in crime. And to the list of reasons assembled by Lutherans and Baptists, it would add three more:

. . . a diminishing sense of responsibility to society, a diminishing sense of self-control, and a diminishing sense of responsibility to God for one's actions.[12]

With insistence, *The Commonweal* would call a halt to the action of the scurrilous press. The space being given in the daily papers to the perennial and unpleasant subject of crime in America is not helping to abate the evil.[13]

The picturesque details which flavor news accounts of bandits and murderers make the peaceful wonder if they may not wake up some morning to find the following advertisement flaunted across a page: "Wanted: healthy, aggressive young men, preferably with a college education, for membership in a highly lucrative crime gang. Commission basis only. Really excellent opportunity for the right type of citizen." [14]

The *America*, contemplating with evident misgivings the heights to which the crime wave will rise before it begins to subside, turns back the pages of history to "the most lawless days of the pioneer West" and is disheartened in the comparison it notes.

The skilled, often highly educated, lawbreakers of today would despise them [bandits of those days] as bungling amateurs. Those simple bandits were satisfied to steal mere thousands. Our modern bandits, it is credibly reported, deal in billions.[15]

Aghast should be the public conscience at figures which indicate that the median age of convicted robbery prisoners is twenty-three years, and even fractionally lower for those who commit burglary.

These ages are testimonials that supervision of parents was sadly lacking at the very age when it should have been most careful.

> Past experience . . . shows that in a majority of . . . cases, the boy came from a home broken by divorce, extreme indigence, or domestic discord. In some instances, however, juvenile delinquents are found in homes in which, while there is no external break, father and mother have time for every interest, except the tremendously important interest of trying to understand and train a growing boy.[16]

Zealously the group would recall to all Catholic parents that the Catholic school is the most powerful auxiliary at their disposal. "The Catholic school is inferior to none in the means it employs to develop the intellect, while in character development it has no peer."[17] The natural virtues are of great value, but of themselves can never form a Christian character. "Only the grace of God building on nature can do that."[18]

It would appear that *The Christian Register*, in its usual tradition, veers slightly right of center, and ventures that one way to stay the avalanche of crime is to enforce law, but, "in our opinion it is not the most important way."[19] In fact, justice must be tempered. Judicial dealing-of-death has become an event of horror for many citizens, and the memory of it haunts ordinary consciences. A life for a life is the rule of the jungle-minded.[20]

> We . . . boast our religion, and our reaching up to heaven with an outstretched arm, while with the other we send to destruction the least of these, the most tragic, our brethren.[21]

In moral and spiritual influence, as much as in the force of civil law and fear of punishment, the Unitarians place their trust. The most daring offenders are young men—not hardened criminals. Had those boys been imbued with the sound influences that emanate from religion, education, and home training, they would not have taken the fatal step on the moral incline.

> It may be that not all of us are prepared to say with the Salvation Army, that no man or woman is so low sunk or in such desperate case, that the gospel of love and hope will not save him . . . but we do believe in the power of these higher influences to start boys and girls right, and keep them right.[22]

The attitude of Methodists is definitely averse to the sentiment evinced by Unitarians in their pleas for the rights of criminals. The denomination of Methodists regards this disposition on the part of so many people as a potent factor in the imperiling of society with the presence and free movement of many vicious criminals.[23]

If a bad man gets into the coils of the law he may depend upon the earnest watchfulness of many good citizens who appoint themselves overseers of justice and insist that he be treated with the utmost kindness and tenderness; that he be given every advantage in selecting the jury and in the presentation of evidence. If he gets convicted, sensitive souls are likely to organize themselves from one side of the land to the other to have the sentence recalled—especially when the case gets to be nationally notorious. People who know nothing at first hand will grow excited of newspaper propagandism and join in a wide agitation and spasm, thinking some poor, innocent person is about to suffer.[24]

The public must be educated concerning the calamities that await the country if crime is allowed to run so high. Officers and juries must be backed up, even braced up. "No time is this to resort to behaviorist philosophies in excuses of vicious youths. Society must fight for its safety, for its decency, and for its life."[25] Society is in a dangerous mood towards itself when it compromises its own rights of safety. The group lets it be known, however, that it is not so naive as to think that jails and gallows are sufficient correctives. "Unbelief and luxury and vanity and loose manners have weakened our moral nature. Carelessness and wilfulness and greed and fun have warped our higher sensibilities."[26] Injured pride may resent but cannot refute the taunt that there is more crime in America than anywhere in the world.

The Northern Conference of Methodists gives evidence that it is agitated by the impetus the press is affording to crime.

So long as the daily newspapers continue to feature stories of crime, so long will such evil expressions of human nature occupy a large place in the thinking and imagination of the public, to the exclusion of more wholesome thoughts and pictures.[27]

These Methodists see but one sordid explanation for the prevalent playing up of crime stories: crime news sells papers. Society cannot wash its own hands of guilt and responsibility in the spreading of crime.[28]

A meeting of the Episcopalian clergy, called to discuss the crime situation, presents to the denomination its banner in the crusade against crime, and the editor of *The Living Church* unfurls it for the fold. The indifference of parents, lack of home life, disrespect for parents, lack of religious training, corrupt public officials and courts, ineffective laws, and moral decadence are points of attack. The home and the Church must be made the fountainheads whence remedies will come.[29]

Lutheran, Catholic, Baptist, and Methodist segments show an understandable perturbation over the matter of narcotics and, in inexorable terms, decry the traffic.

The problem, in the estimate of the Missouri Synod of Lutherans, has reached a stage which must demand serious consideration of parents, pastors, educators, and all charged with the responsibility of training youth.[30]

The Catholic group, whose voice becomes articulate in the editorial offices of *The Commonweal*, would ask for more than community consideration—it dictates concerted action.

> The narcotic habit proves more destructive each year; and though sometimes its famous victims—literary men, cinema stars, sons and daughters of the wealthy—bring the monster "dope" before the public, co-ordinated action against it makes slow progress.[31]

The sinister traffic must be "cleaned up."

> Now, just as in the time of Francis Thompson, many people do not realize that children are brought up in sin from their cradles, that they knew evil before they knew good, that the boys are ruffians and profligates, the girls, harlots in the mother's womb.[32]

Sober solicitude likewise colors the vocalization of Baptist opinion. This huge increase in the use of drugs will avenge not only addicts but future generations with deleterious results. Especially repugnant to decency and morality are figures showing that young people between the ages of eighteen and twenty-five are held in the tentacles of the vicious habit.[33] That today the narcotic traffic is a menace second to nothing imperiling the manhood and womanhood of the nation, is the considered comment of *The Baptist*.

> Since the war and largely due to the war and to the commercial greed to make money out of the impulse on the part of nerve-shattered individuals to drown consciousness with a drug, has the traffic grown.[34]

The general apathy of the public is to be regretted, asserts the Southern Conference of Methodists. Many decades were required to create a national conscience on liquor, it ruefully admits, but hopes that "surely the country will much more easily rise up and slay the traffic in narcotics."[35] There must be an ironclad law that will prohibit the manufacture in the United States of more than the infinitesimal quantity absolutely required for medicinal purposes.[36] Obviously it is hard to cope with drug smugglers, "but to admit that the government cannot cope with them and put a stop to their nefarious business is to admit an impotency that we do not believe is true of the American government."[37]

With aimed invective against those who claim that the wider use of narcotics is due to the prohibition law, the voice of Methodists of the Northern Conference seems to stamp its foot as it levels its accusations. "Saloonists start the specious report that former users of alcohol are becoming drug addicts."[38] Investigation shows such assertions to have no foundation in fact, answer fellow Methodists in the South. In practically every instance, victims of the drug habit are young men and women, often in their teens. Rarely are they alcoholics.[39] Agreeing that this is true, Northern Methodists are nonetheless quick to retort that "the gullibility of the good is an established fact. Numbers of persons who . . . prayed for prohibition, weakly collapse when confronted by the bold assertions that the saloonists make. . . ."[40]

Thus the religious journals thought and spoke as regards the traffic in narcotics. There remains for us now to consider the third aspect of the wave of lawlessness—a relatively small rivulet but threatening to widen into a dangerous current—student suicides. The equanimity of Catholics, Lutherans, Methodists, Baptists, Presbyterians, and Unitarians is ruffled by the gathering momentum of the evil.

In January, 1927 seven college students took their own lives. This distressing record calls forth comment of opinion on the part of Catholics. The *America*, voicing the group's attitude, would remind everyone that unless proper training is tendered youth in its perilous years, mental and moral disorders are inevitable. Glancing back on the life histories of the above-mentioned college students, the periodical tarries over the paths along which some of these unfortunate boys wandered to self-murder. In one case, the lad "reaped the bitter fruit of parental neglect, plus a course at school and college which did nothing to build up character."[41]

In two other cases, courses at school and college, which completely eliminated God from life's equation, taught these youths to conclude that since the equation had no answer it were wiser to abandon the problem by ending life.[42]

The group admits an inexpressible sadness as it contemplates the baneful influence to which young people are exposed. On every side danger is lurking, while the home and school afford a deplorably weak protection.

Parental neglect and a system of education from which religion and morality are divorced are reproducing the massacre of the innocents on an infinitely larger scale than in the days of King Herod.[43]

Writing in the same year and with the same record before it, the group of United Lutherans wonders if suicide among students has reached a point where it can be an epidemic. Judging the present in the light of the past, Lutherans grimly recall that weakness in faith and character is ever more evident in days of prosperity than in times of adversity.[44] The home is lax in developing character.

Perhaps if children were disciplined into enduring a little hardness for the right development of Christian character there would be fewer suicides when they are older. But great is the power of suggestion when there is no sustaining and uplifting faith to meet life's weariness.[45]

Methodists try to calm their own apprehensions by "whistling in the dark," as it were. The unusually large number of suicides occurring in 1921—more than twenty thousand—are probably, in large part, due to the reactions of the war on the nervous and mental constitutions. But the attempt to quiet their fears has failed, for there is a fact which cannot be explained to their satisfaction by war reaction. In the three year period, 1919-1921, the number of suicides among youths has increased nearly one hundred per cent. Figures give the facts: "There were 477 in 1919, 707 in 1920, and 858 in 1921."[46]

Over a period of six years, the disquietude has not been allayed. The record of suicides in the first months of 1927 harasses the waking hours of this group, as it has those of the Lutherans and Catholics. A variety of causes has been put forth as contributory to this disgraceful account:

Laxity of home discipline, shallow views of life, poor religious training, nervous speed of life, confusion in the thinking of the present time, materialistic influences, inability to meet hardship or disappointment and the demands for thrills.[47]

"Yes," the Methodists agree, "these, any or all, may have their part to play in the explanation. Might not also the disposition of young people to go in gangs have something to do with these suicides?"[48] The gang spirit does not solve the problem entirely either, the group would answer to its own query—but it cannot be altogether overlooked. A shining example is set, and imitators follow it. Indeed, youth must be taught to dare to be different.[49]

The curtain of tragedy is drawn back by Baptists of the Northern Convention and the reading public is made familiar with some intimacies—pregnant with meaning—in a recent suicide. The story runs thus. A young woman, twenty years of age, rebuked for lack of punctuality by her father, took her own life. A note left behind assuring her mother that "you have been the best mother, every bit that the word *mother* signifies,"[50] was signed "Baby."

For the Baptists, the signature of the note is the significant feature. In the word *Baby* is hidden the secret of the mother's failure to do anything more than "baby" the child she brought into the world. The daughter's act carries in itself condemnation for the kind of mothering which leaves an adult daughter at the mercy of her childishness. There are far too many of these "babies" in the world. Behind the appearance of an adult they hide the soul of a two-year old.[51]

> Whimpering over pain, weeping over every disappointment, resenting life's stern discipline they are the despair of their friends and a perpetual irritant to all their acquaintances.[52]

It is certainly unfair for a mother to leave her child naked and defenseless against the world. She owes to that child the discipline which makes for character and self-control.[53]

The wave of student suicides passing over the country is a distressing but not an unprecedented fact in the minds of Presbyterians who are articulate through the medium of *The Presbyterian Banner*.

> When a morbid idea gets rooted in a group it may become an obsession and work like an epidemic. In the Middle Ages a wave of children's suicides spread over Europe and hundreds of young children destroyed themselves. The fact that members of their own class are

doing a thing may act as an unconscious but powerful suggestion on other members to do the same thing.[54]

This religious segment agrees that this does not entirely allay the alarm of the situation that runs counter to all the energies and hopes usually associated with youth. Specific causes are impossible to catalogue, the Presbyterians hold. Nevertheless, one general cause might safely be cited: disillusionment which follows on the heels of a materialistic view of life.[55] "The bottom falls out of life under such philosophy. The game does not seem worth the candle and why not snuff it out?"[56] Only a deeper foundation of faith in the eternal things of the spirit can cure and prevent such a pessimistic background that leads inevitably to such tragic results.[57]

Some probing into the life histories of two young women, victims of their own destruction, leads the Unitarians to speak their thoughts. The one from a wealthy family "chose companionship in the perfumed atmosphere where the rights of the senses are sanctified with rotten sophistries;"[58] the other, a product of the slums, "pursued the dark ways of life, craving expression after the sodden manner of her foul but hypocritical environment."[59] Cruel disaster ended the lives of both. "Two girls, two origins, and one destiny. America, this is not a good advertisement for you!"[60]

The wave of lawlessness—just as so many another manifestation of the revolt of the postwar decade—had not spent itself when the decade closed. With the dawn of the Thirties, however, other pressing matters tended to crowd out many items which had alarmed the public in the Twenties. True it is that in the 1920's the "crime wave" was one of the most common topics in news and editorial comment. "And yet it is still an open question whether there was a crime wave, in the sense of an absolute increase in the total volume of law violation."[61]

Statistics were in such a confused and unreliable condition that one might well be wary in arriving at airtight conclusions. Perhaps, what appeared to contemporary society as a real increase in lawlessness was merely a shift to newer forms of crime. Perhaps, too, notoriety and publicity jarred proportions into chaos and bewilderment. But it cannot be gainsaid that the general low moral tone of the Twenties offered weak opposition when the flood gates swayed dangerously in their watery foundations.

"And will you, being a man of good breeding, be married under a bush, like a beggar? Get you to a church and have a good priest that can tell you what marriage is."

—William Shakespeare, *As You Like It.*

CHAPTER X

Wanton Wickedness

The fact that William Shakespeare, writing in the year 1598, should demand a definite, sacred surrounding for marriage, might indicate for some, a certain antiquity and venerability for the matrimonial ritual. The truth, of course, is that the origin of the sacredness surrounding marriage goes back to the Garden of Eden. And it is probably true that ever since that time there have appeared, at more or less frequent intervals, Cassandras holding out but little hope for the endurance not only of the ritual but also of the very institution of marriage itself. The elders of every age have thought their youths the worst generation ever. A cuneiform fragment found amid the ruins of Babylon bears this ever ancient, ever new comment: "Alas! Alas! times are not what they used to be."[1] And in 1817, a certain lady writing about the youths of her day said: "Nothing like the young people of today has ever been seen. They make one's hair stand on end. They have neither manners nor morals."[2]

Hence, it is not surprising that the 1920's should hear billowy and booming thunderings on all sides. The years were ones strongly seasoned with fun and frivolity—ones in which the time-honored moral code was apparently receiving vigorous tremors.

The institution of marriage seemed to be threatened by the so-called "companionate unions." The phrase was first generally publicized by Judge Benjamin B. Lindsey, whose services in the juvenile court of Denver, Colorado, had convinced him that conventional marriage laws were being increasingly disregarded by the rising generation. In 1927 he proposed to establish companionate marriage on a legal basis and thereupon opened a barrage of opposition.

The trend was evidently on the increase through the decade. In 1925 a sociologist declared: "Our United States family . . . is monogamic in form with an apparent tendency toward term marriage, and what is coming to be called companionate marriage."[3]

Although statistics would seem to indicate that the marriage rate was fairly constant, the mere fact that the companionate marriage was so seriously debated shows that the older views and habits regarding marriage did not go unchallenged.

The Unitarians, in a tone of unnecessary apology, tendered wholehearted support to one of their ministers who officiated at such a marriage. "If we are the Experimentalists in religion, as distinguished from the Fundamentalists . . . why should we not experiment?"[4] Their own position is unequivocal. They see nothing "shocking" about a companionate marriage.

> On the contrary . . . it is a fact, practiced already by thousands of persons whose situation, in their own conscience and discretion, does not justify them at present to enter into a family marriage.[5]

The institution of marriage with its wreckage strewn all over the land is the most tragic commentary on our barbaric ignorance of the proper relations of male and female. "There is no subject in life about which we are such moral cowards as the subject of sex. . . . Experimentation, it seems to us, cannot make our social order worse."[6]

The group thinks it is the time to stop the prurient bashfulness which has wrought its worst on home and children, men and women, and in this respect made America probably the lowest morally of any civilized nation.[7]

> Why not try intelligence and candor? Christian, our standards? No. In marriage, as in every other practice and doctrine, America is prevailingly Fundamentalist.[8]

The unmollified denunciation of what religious leaders are naming "unmarried unions" and "sex experiments" is, in the minds of the Unitarians, indicative of two things: an utter lack of comprehension of the way the mind of youth works, and an equal lack of knowledge of the proper way to apply Christianity.[9] Those against whom condemnatory manifestos of disapproval are aimed will first ridicule and then entirely disregard them. "One fact is with us," the group goes on to affirm, "and all the invective and denunciation we can volley against it will not alter it; namely, that young people are looking at life through entirely different eyes."[10]

New interpretations of freedom, humanism, behaviorism, and numerous other modern influences are creating a distinctly new and original type of mind. One-time offenses against the proprieties are no longer offenses. It is not enough for parents to say, "Don't do it!" They must give adequate reasons. Young people today are looking for truth as well as thrills, and are utilizing methods for finding the former as for procuring the latter, which are not justified by the fathers, but are justified according to the psychology of the behaviorists. Such motives as self-denial, discipline, and obedience weigh but lightly in the balance against self-expression and independence.[11]

This denominational group is of a mind that it makes but little difference whether the changes are liked or disliked; their actuality is with us. Unitarians do not want to appear as advocating "unmarried unions" and "sex experiments," but maintain intrepidly that they desire to see the world and the lure of life as youth views it. Any doubt still lurking as to the position of the segment is dissolved by the reiteration of their policy in brisk, unbending words:

An entirely new sense of what is right and what is wrong is developing, and we make bold to add, ought to develop. . . . Some things are naturally attractive and some things are repulsive. Nothing short of a miracle makes them otherwise. Some things are beautiful, and some things are ugly. The fact that some things are attractive, beautiful, and of good report is going to determine their acceptance by future generations, rather than that they conform to a moral code imposed on mankind some centuries ago.[12]

Episcopalians claim that the subject "which is now sweetly termed 'companionate marriages' is old, and quite old. These unions are excursions into relationships that smack of Neanderthal culture."[13] Only the name is new.

Sitting in judgment on the parents of a couple who recently entered upon a marriage of this nature, *The Living Church* borrows chill terms.

. . . The bride's parents talk as if a great and wonderful experiment were about to be tried. They speak of a "more rational life," and "a human agreement admitting the possibility of failure." Fancy phrases aside, the couple have decided to get a divorce if love fails them. So they start with neither the thrill of confidence nor the joy of struggle, of making their way unassisted. And we have been told that the new, flaming youth is as original, bold and defiant as Lucifer! This synthetic "companionate" stuff is as daring as a kitten drinking a saucer of milk under its mother's guidance.[14]

In February of 1927, an eminent and qualified spokesman for the religious group publicly protests against the type of marriage advocated by Judge Lindsey and his followers. The moral standards, the Bishop persists, have been given to the world by Christ and are not open to debate. In spite of any and all assertions to the contrary, the temporary, so-called "companionate marriage" is not a marriage but only another name for free love. Any teachings to the contrary lead not forward but backward to those conditions which destroyed the old pagan world.[15]

An Episcopalian rector who reportedly placed himself in the camp of those favoring "unmarried unions and all the rest of the new morality" is highly commended by the official organ of the Unitarians. Indirectly, the commendations indicate the uncompromising position of the Episcopal group. He has met the situation in society as it should be met—contending that "we must make our own standards, as each age has done."[16]

This rector has principles which seem sound to the mind of the Unitarians and they do not hesitate to adopt them.

What makes the independence and impatience of youth is a creative determination by them that what their fathers did was not good enough for a growing world in which they are the upcoming representatives. If the home as we know it does not produce the best results on the individual and society, then let us do something to the home.[17]

The Episcopalian clergyman is quoted. His tenets cannot be gainsaid.

If to sanctify unmarried unions would do away with promiscuity, and the double standards, and better protect the children of legal marriages . . . then to keep on fussing with . . . the idea that all marriages are made in heaven, is utter folly.[18]

The Unitarians are decisively unsympathetic with the church of which this rector is a member. "Its leadership is in the hands of Fundamentalists. It cannot be expected to have an open mind on the social application of the gospel when it has a closed mind on the gospel itself!"[19]

A marriage of a temporary nature, to be adopted as a finality or dissolved after a trial, was the subject of an interview with some university students and the results of this please *The Presbyterian Banner*. The sentiments expressed in the characteristic language of young men and women "have the right ring and strike true to fundamental ideas and ideals."[20]

The whole idea of companionate marriage as it is viewed by the "liberal" Presbyterians is repugnant to Christian principles, based on false psychology, and contains in itself the seeds of its own dissolution.[21]

The same group has nothing but sharp words of reproof for Judge Lindsey who, "once had the respect of his city," but now "he has fallen far."[22] This theory of companionate marriage which the Judge defines as marriage "with divorce by mutual consent," when attended with birth control is simply "licensed sexuality terminable at will of either party."[23] It is based on the impermanence of sexuality, is repugnant to Christian ethics, and is fatal to the family.[24]

Catholics, in their periodicals, thoughtfully rap out their convictions on this problem. The *America* notes that:

> . . . none of Lindsey's theories and suggested practices are new. They are as old as sin itself. But generally they have been acted upon in secret and with a sense of shame; it remains to our day to offer them as remedies for some of our gravest social disorders.[25]

These theories are really attempts to destroy sex immorality by legitimating it. They outrage some of the holiest memories of every decent-thinking man. They cannot be reconciled with what most Americans are old-fashioned enough to call "morality."[26]

The editorial columns of *The Commonweal* have coldly measured tones to describe the attitude of the Catholics for whom it speaks. Their ire, early in 1927, is heightened by a report of a "free union" which ended in a murder and a suicide but, fearing that their anger may exceed proper limits, they permit themselves but "mild wonder at the misnomer that ever labeled such unions 'free' at all."[27]

> Only the congenital moron is deceived by the sophistry today. Others know that no enslavement is so complete, and no situation so beset by peril, as that of the woman who has entered into a union of whose endurance passion is the only guarantor and law "outside the law" the sole protection.[28]

Later in the same year, a playwright produced a play "that dares to tell the young to learn life first and marry afterwards."[29] Again, the editorial staff of *The Commonweal* fairly bristles against "that select brood who believe that God was just a little old-fashioned when He provided the mating instinct with its natural consequence of child birth."[30] The group reviews the amazing human fallacy underlying the whole argument about companionate marriage, and wonders how one can possibly "learn life" before accepting the responsibilities of life. "Life and marriage cannot be learned in what is only the primer of sex."[31] Stripped of sentimental phrases, companionate marriage can do but one thing: gratify the senses without ratifying the judgment.

> It cannot even evoke the crucial test of character which comes with facing the issue of permanent responsibility—of living in "chains," whether they be chains of love, of compromise or merely of manly and womanly duty.[32]

In short, direct terms the Catholics would recall to all some very basic notions.

> Minus a promise to abide by the rules of the game and play it to the end; without frank acceptance of marriage as an institution merging two individuals in one unity; without finally, any realization that acceptance of the Divine Will is the threshold to a satisfactory and blessed life—without all these things, matrimony is only a legally dignified "affair." [33]

Toward the end of 1928 Catholic opinion regards the excitement over companionate marriage as happily subsiding. "Contrary alike to Christian concepts and to any valid concept of domestic society, the 'companionate' will probably be practiced only by those whose morals are either undeveloped or corrupt."[34]

Very cleverly and with a rhetorical flourish the Northern Conference of Methodists describes an open debate between Judge Lindsey and a certain pastor of a Methodist Episcopal Church under the similitude of a bullfight. The Methodist clergyman, a gallant but inexorable matador, after several onslaughts finally disposed of the bull.[35]

The Methodists were not a whit surprised at the outcome of the forensic bullfight but

> what does amaze us is that a proposal like that of the Denver judge, which encourages immorality by making it legal, strikes at the heart of the Christian home, and lays the ax at the root of the Anglo-Saxon

social system, can command the attention of the American people, even for an hour.[36]

This section of Methodists would emphatically admonish all not to be misled by terms. "Unmarried unions" is just another "velvety phrase" for the old-fashioned "burlap word, fornication."[37]

Somehow the use of the older word seems to conduce to clearer thinking and saner judgment. If Judge Ben Lindsey had written fornication or free love into the phrasing of his proposal for "companionate marriage," it would probably have died before it was born. Calling a spade a spade saves errors. . . . [38]

The Lutherans of the Missouri Synod are disgusted with the nauseous talk of companionate marriage.[39] The term has been invented merely to camouflage the latest attack of the devil upon the institution of marriage. The name *marriage* cannot be applied to such a union because marriage is for life. The group even entertains serious doubts, if it came to a legal test, that the companionate marriage would be sustained as a valid marriage relation.

The partners to it live in concubinage, which is a polite word where another, in fact, several others, could be used. A sexual relation . . . entered into with the express understanding that abortion or preventive perversities will be practiced lacks an essential element of the marriage contract. No polite words about "changed economic conditions," "the problem of emotional compulsion," etc., can cover up the extreme nastiness of the affair. . . . [40]

The voice of the United Lutherans is just as outraged as the above group about the new thought and free love "in this our day" when "Mormonism is being put to the blush by a class of well-fed and well-groomed men who go about 'plucking the blush of innocence from off the cheek of maidenhood and putting a blister there.' "[41] On the whole, the Lutherans sense, there is a distressful looseness of thinking and sentiment on the question of marriage. And Judge Lindsey must bear the responsibility for a great part of it despite his expressing himself as being opposed to "free love" and to the so-called "trial marriage." His statements of defense are "as weak as water and far less refreshing."[42] He places himself under just suspicion by suggesting as a possible remedy for illicit sex relationships and the terrible evils growing out of them, what is known as "companionate marriage." This is a subterfuge and intimately related to "free love."[43] The Judge, it would seem, inclines to advise youth to choose the lesser of two evils dealing with the sex problem. This is "a purely naturalistic method."[44] The logical consequences of such teaching, Lutherans hold, cannot but impress man that he is first and foremost an animal, with animal instincts and passions. Man then will but wonder why the Christian code of marital ethics should be enforced upon him.[45]

The three Baptist journals examined in this study, likewise have opinions which they are anxious to express. Northern Baptists do not appear too agitated over the matter. With evident attempts at a deliberate calm they would shrug off the problem as inconsequential: in millions of American homes the proposal of trial marriage does not awaken the slightest personal interest. Those are the homes where husband and wife have entered voluntarily into a lifelong union from which they wish no release. For those to whom marriage becomes a trial through a lack of understanding, Northern Baptists would advocate more than simply turning it into a trial marriage.[46]

The Southern Conference of Baptists regrets that Judge Lindsey, who for more than twenty years was one of our noted national figures, should now be playing the fool.[47]

> He became possessed with the belief that religion and the basic foundation of virtue and home are not main essentials. He became half crazed with some social Utopia which could, he thought, be reached in a way that did not go by the Cross and take in the Commandments. . . . There are no reforms—no social programs—no expert theories that can work the redemption of mankind when we leave out religion and the sanctity of the home.[48]

His preaching of free love is breaking down the old standard foundations of life that have been our bulwark.

In his parting word of the old year, as it were, the editor of *The Watchman-Examiner* in late December of 1927, in a voice that sounds slightly irritated, soliloquizes on the position of *The Christian Register* in the matter of companionate marriage. He frankly sees little, if any, grounds for pride on the part of Unitarians in their vaunted "liberalism." In 1928, he is still distressed when he considers that one of the worst aspects of companionate marriage is its putting around free love the cloak of respectability.[49]

The only group which does not express itself directly, either favorably or unfavorably, regarding the contemporary marital discussion is the Reform Jewish element. In 1927, the year when Judge Lindsey was under the most severe attack from practically all sections except that of Unitarians, *The American Hebrew* is deeply moved that the Judge has lost his seat in the Juvenile Court due to some legal technicality. It lauds him as one who has helped toward a better understanding of youth.[50]

Judge Lindsey and his followers, as has been seen, stirred up a small cyclonic tempest. His so-called companionate marriage, however, was but one phase of a triple attack launched against the institution of marriage by those who seemed to think that it was time for the ancient and sacred code of marital morals to totter to ruin. Birth control and divorce are the other legs of the tripod from which would-be moderns aimed their volleys. It is to these that we will turn in the next two chapters.

"In our time all Greece was visited by a dearth of children . . . and a failure of productiveness followed . . . by our men's becoming perverted to a passion . . . and the pleasure of an idle life, and accordingly either not marrying, or, if they did marry, refusing to rear children, . . . or at most one or two out of a great number. . . ."

—Polybius, *circa* 150 B. C.

CHAPTER XI

Phantom Parade

Silhouetted against the sky line a phantom parade passes by. The vanguard may have drifted off into the mist of memory, but on and on the procession goes across the horizon of the 1920's, ever increasing its ranks. To many of the religious leaders and spokesmen sitting on the reviewing platform, this phantom parade of souls, denied the gift of life through the practices of birth control, becomes the funeral march of the nation. To others, it apparently assumed the characteristics of a cavalcade of progress of the country.

True it is that contraception, while a particular curse to the decade, was not peculiar to that generation alone, as a quick reference to Genesis will readily confirm.[1] But the steadily declining birth rate in the 1920's was an undeniable fact and attested in large part to the momentum that the birth control movement was gaining.

The American Birth Control League, organized in 1917, and spearheaded by Margaret Sanger, "the Mother of Planned Parenthood," carried on an active propaganda during the Twenties. In the pages of a magazine called *The Woman Rebel*, Mrs. Sanger used the phrase "birth control" for the first time. The initial issue was barred from the mails, but its author incorporated its information in a booklet entitled *Family Limitation*. She then left for Europe to avoid arrest, having ordered copies to be distributed after her departure.

Returning to the United States in 1921 she opened the first birth control clinic in the country in Brooklyn, New York. In ten days the law intervened and closed the institution. However, in 1923, the courts of New York ruled that physicians might legally give contraceptive information for reasons of health. Mrs. Sanger now, under the auspices of Dr. Hannah M. Stone, opened a permanent clinic in New York City, and later in many other cities, although in some states they were not permitted.[2]

Such were the beginnings of the organized movement that so violently rocked the foundations of the home in the Twenties, and our editors of the religious journals readily took "sides" in the discussion of it. Lutherans and Catholics are uncompromising in their opposition. Sections of Methodists, Baptists, Episcopalians, and Unitarians are either tolerant or favorable. Presbyterians, by action later during the 1930's, it would seem, oppose it. The Reform Jewish segment is noncommittal.

The Lutherans of the Missouri Synod bewail the perverse age when the state of motherhood, once so highly prized by the daughters of Israel and among our own ancestors, is, by and large, losing its fascination for the women of the day.

> Bearing and rearing of children is no longer deemed conducive to health, ease, comfort, and the enjoyment of pleasure. . . . If, by accident, a child arrives, it must, most usually, grow up without a mother's love; it is entrusted to the care of strangers.[3]

These unnatural conditions fortunately do not flourish universally but there is an alarming tendency in that direction. Contamination can spread rapidly.

The slogan "Fewer and Better Babies" is winning adherents even in homes where children are still desired. Definitely, the Missouri Synod sees grave danger ahead.[4]

The United Lutherans are convinced that the love of man and wife needs the cementing bond of love for the child. No married life is complete without children. "Many a childless home pays the penalty for its aversion to having offspring in conjugal infidelity and unhappiness."[5] No Christian civilization is possible where the pagan view of a sensualized marriage prevails. "Rome in the last graspings of her earthly power should teach for all time the lesson of what the sensualization of the marriage estate leads to. . . ."[6]

Lutherans of the Missouri Synod, with pride they consider decidedly justifiable, ask, in the spring of 1924, to tell a little story. They preface their tale with a comment that they have no desire, in the present instance, to argue about "a movement [which] advocates the use of drugs and contrivances by which married people and others may 'cheat nature.' "[7] Such a movement can only be devil-inspired. And now their story. A layman of their denomination when traveling through Canada in the recent past read a comment in a daily paper to the effect that a Catholic priest, in the course of some remarks on the subject of race suicide, had said few churches "have the courage to stand out against the latest sin of the age."[8] Whereupon, the Lutheran layman courteously informed him that "the Lutherans of the Missouri Synod have always, as far back as I can remember (I am fifty-one), taken a very decided stand on this subject."[9] The Canadian Jesuit replied that his principal acquaintance had been with the Episcopalian Church, some of whose high dignitaries "have recently used language which can only mean approval of artificial methods of birth restriction."[10] And he added that

it was pleasant to be told that what is evidently an important religious association, the Missouri Synod, has expressed itself so emphatically on the right side.[11]

This religious group graciously accepts the compliment.

What have Catholics to say? The group which voices its sentiments through the *America* categorically presents its position.

According to the teaching of Catholic theologians, deliberately to frustrate, or to attempt to frustrate, the normal operation of the faculties intended for procreation, is a violation of the natural law and is grievously sinful. There can be no possible compromise with this frightful evil.[12]

To the question of well-intentioned non-Catholics as to whether the Church will not some day change her attitude, the answer is in the negative.

The Church has no jurisdiction over the natural law, save such as is implied in her office to defend, formulate, and interpret it. God, the Creator of all that exists, and not the Church of God, is the Author of the natural law. The Church cannot repeal that law, nor can she change its essence or extent by omission or addition.[13]

These Catholics stoutly assert that they are well aware "that abstention from unnatural practice [of birth control] sometimes calls for a moral strength scarcely less than heroic."[14] The hero is the man who dares to attempt what his fellows call the impossible.

Fidelity to God's decree that the nature which He has made must be respected, may be difficult, as truth, chastity, loyalty, the magnificent willingness to suffer the loss of all things but honor, may also be difficult. But none of them is impossible. . . . And the Catholic Church, teaching that by the grace of a merciful and all-loving God, man can rise to unvisioned heights of sanctity, points to uncounted sons and daughters who in every age have deemed goodness better than comfort, and death more desirable than sin.[15]

Not birth control but self-control is needed for the true welfare of the individual and the general good of the State.

Putting aside reasons based on moral principles for a moment, this group considers that the sharp decrease in the birth rate of a country rich in natural resources is an ominous sign of national decay.[16] "Unhallowed interference with the law which Almighty God has written in our very nature . . . is certain to entail fearful results to any community in which it becomes common."[17] All the fearful prophecies of an overcrowded country made by amateur propagandists "run smack against the scientific conclusions of population experts who faintly whisper 'bunk.' "[18] Ripe, indeed, is the time for these experts to speak a little louder.

> Granting full recognition to the purity of their [birth control advocates'] motives, it remains true that they are enemies not only of good morals but, by necessary consequence, of the State.[19]

The laymen in the editorial offices of *The Commonweal* hasten to inform all that their constituents give a hearty nod of approval to sentiments stated by the *America*. Their first statement is as startling as paradoxical: "The Church does not condemn birth control."[20] The declaration is elucidated.

> Indeed, by its teaching on virginal and conjugal chastity it has exercised such an effective birth control that Malthus' gloomy prophecies were never fulfilled. But the Church has no authority to approve anything merely masquerading as birth control, when this thing is lust-uncontrol.[21]

These Catholics in what they term "plain English" are anxious to reiterate a few basic and fundamental facts.

> If a man and a woman wish to have the sacrament of marriage they can have it on certain conditions. If they do not wish to have the sacrament they need not have it. The conditions of a Christian marriage are that the marriage act shall be used for begetting children. If the man and woman intend to seek sterile venereal satisfaction with the help of chemical or mechanical appliances, this is not marriage. It is a form of harlotry, which keeps the old Christian name of marriage.[22]

Birth control is wrong, not because the Church declares it to be sinful, but because it is a violation of the natural law. Hence, the position of the Church is adamant and unyielding. "Some acts are wrong merely because they are forbidden; others are forbidden because they are wrong in themselves, and to this second class birth control belongs."[23] The Church should not be accused of claiming autocratic power in this matter of neo-Malthusian birth control. "She rests her action on the principle—*non possumus*: we cannot."[24]

Momentarily *The Commonweal*, just as the *America*, considers the problem of population decrease on the score of other than a moral issue. The unscientific fear of the unborn which so greatly troubled the mind of "that Anglican divine, Mr. Malthus," has assumed the proportions of a stampede.[25] Birth control has argued a bad case on the basis of insufficient and faulty generalization from random facts. "America does not sensibly fear the unborn. It may reasonably be anxious about the vacancies in the ranks of the born."[26]

With a touch of infinite irony and in an evident chuckling undertone, the editor of *The Commonweal* cannot resist a jab at those preachers of birth control who vaunt that they will destroy the tradition of organized Christianity.

> It is interesting to learn that the tradition of organized Christianity, that survived the power of Nero, the prestige of Julian, the genius of Voltaire, and the apocalypse of the French Revolution, is now to be smashed; and if we knew where this ceremony is appointed to take place, we should like to go and see it.[27]

Terms employed in the discussion of birth control by contraception are ambiguous and not clearly defined. Usually the disputants are not in accord as to the meaning of the issues involved. This, in the opinion of the Episcopalians, accounts for the fact that the air is not being cleared by debate. The word *unnatural* is a case in point. To the birth control advocate it may mean *artificial* or *repulsive*, or it may contain both meanings. To his opponent, "in accord with Latin moral theology, . . . it is 'a perversion of nature,' in which 'the faculty is so used that it cannot attain its primary end. . . . The faculty is compelled to defeat itself.' "[28]

Readers are left to draw their own conclusions by the Episcopalian group, but not so by the Unitarians. To these, birth control simply means the application of intelligence to the birth rate. "Not only is the quantity of our human stock interesting; even more so is its quality."[29] An attempt is made to clarify some of the issues involved. Birth control is in the interests of a larger and better life. It is brought about by the prevention of conception, not by interference of life that has begun. It advocates children coming by choice and not by chance. Children can thus be spaced according to the ability of parents to provide for them. For those who object to birth control on the grounds that it is unnatural, the Unitarians have a ready retort.

> Of course it is. All of our life is unnatural. We could not now live under absolutely natural conditions. Electric lights, and all other sorts of electrical devices are artificial. Most of the food we eat is the result of artificially selected seeds and crossing, producing species which are very different from the originals.[30]

A Unitarian group scheduled to hold a meeting in a certain hall was barred when it was learned that there was to be a discussion on birth control. Several other halls were placed at the disposal of the ousted group. This news item drew comments in *The Christian Register* and, by inference, indicated the direction of the thinking of several other denominations on contraception since two meeting places controlled by Methodists opened to the group and a Baptist church informed the Unitarians that "they could not speak of birth control under its roof."[31] Of course, all-embracing conclusions cannot be drawn, for it may be that the decisions were made on the personal opinion of the ministers involved.

Neither the Northern nor Southern Baptist journals enters the verbal fray. The organ supposedly representing interests of all members of the denomination, *The Watchman-Examiner,* has a few remarks to make. The editor seems to be in a hostile mood as he pens his comments. The caustic vein evident here is unusual and has not marked the utterances on other subjects. He apparently has daggers drawn against some of the Catholic clergy and their church for some condemnatory statements against birth control.

> The oldest, strongest, and most autocratic body known, a body that compels "birth control" all over the world, is the Roman hierarchy. The choice young men of the church, trained as priests, are forced into celibacy; called "Father," indeed, but denied the joy of fatherhood. Their choice young women, trained as nuns, are forced into a life that denies them motherhood. Behold a great body, that assumes to be the

Church, stabbing birth control! For a thousand years and more it has forced its chosen leaders to practice birth control.[32]

It seems fairly evident, however, that the above satire sprang from a personal slant and can scarcely be interpreted as expressive of Baptists' unqualified approval of contraception. This fact seems to be borne out in editorial comment made two years later. The group is discussing a certain eminent minister of the extreme "liberal" wing and his favoring scientific birth control. God's command "Be fruitful, and multiply, and replenish the earth" hardly admits of scientific interpretation, as far as *The Watchman-Examiner* views the Biblical text. Then, cynically, the journal constructs what the minister's comment to this objection would probably be.

When God gave that advice, there were only two persons in the world, whereas now the population has grown to almost unnumbered millions, and unless scientific birth control is inaugurated, the time is coming when somebody will be crowded clear off the earth, to say nothing about many of the rest being unable to find enough to eat.[33]

The Baptist magazine concludes that possibly the logic of the argument would be this. "Since God did not think about that in the beginning, He cannot be trusted to control the matter now."[34]

The American Birth Control League receives an encomium from Methodists of the Northern Conference.

It is the name of a group of earnest women and men, whose laudable zeal for the welfare of the race has led them to advocate the artificial limitation of births. The idea . . . has not made rapid progress in America, though a few have advocated it with apostolic fervor by voice and pen.[35]

The same group is vexed over what they term "police control" rather than "birth control." A recent public meeting in New York City, sponsored in the interest of birth control, was dispersed by the police. In general, the public is not vitally bothered about the issue under discussion, the Methodists would strongly vouch, but it is extremely interested in what constitutes human freedom. "It is shocked wide awake to learn that reputable citizens can be molested in their right of free assembly."[36] Since report has it that a Catholic prelate was the force behind police action, the group is rather curt and states that "civil liberty is in danger when any policeman . . .

takes orders from a Protestant minister or a Catholic monsignor without due warrant of law."[37]

Protestant churchmen, it is obvious, disagreed among themselves on the moral issues involved in the matter of birth control. In 1930, the Committee on Marriage and the Home of the Federal Council of Churches recommended that

> . . . the Church should not seek to impose its point of view as to the use of contraceptives upon the public by legislation or any other form of coercion; and especially should not seek to prohibit physicians from imparting such information to those who in the judgment of the medical profession are entitled to receive it.[38]

The statement was criticized by the General Assembly of the Presbyterian Church as dangerous to morals.

The Roman Catholic Church did not deviate from her uncompromising position. A papal encyclical, *Casti Connubii*, was issued by Pope Pius XI in 1930, in which the Pontiff described contraceptive devices as an "offence against the law of God and of nature."[39]

As the epoch drew to a close it could not be denied that the day of the fractional (and fractious) household had not only dawned but also had come to stay. A magazine writer lamented that "having a family is not an American ideal." A family of two or three children became the national standard.[40] Gone indeed into the mists of memory were former records like the following. Benjamin Franklin was the eighth among ten children; William Sherman, the sixth among eleven; Horace Greeley was one of seven; Longfellow, one of eight; Washington Irving was the tenth child; Beethoven was one of a family of eleven, as was General Pershing.

One is tempted to speculate as to what the loss to the world would have been if any or all of these had been in the phantom parade. But to speculate thus is beyond the province and ken of the historian!

"Oh, why should vows so fondly made
Be broken ere the morrow?"

—James Hoog, *The Broken Heart.*

CHAPTER XII

Broken Bonds

A few miles beyond the confines of Paris, in a lovely sylvan re-
treat, stands the old home of Napoleon and Josephine.
The tourist finds the furniture in Napoleon's room just as it
was when the First Consul planned his brilliant and spectacular campaigns which led to his renowned triumphs at Marengo, Austerlitz,
Jena, and the Pyramids—victories which remade the map of Europe.
A feminine touch still hovers over the room of Josephine. Incidentals
here and there echo notes of devotion. In the center of the room
stands a harp on which, in the days of their happiness, Josephine
strummed lyrics of love. Now it is mute. Its strings are broken.
To an author who recently visited this home, the torn strings on
that harp were depictive of

a broken home, a family torn asunder, a sacred vow trampled under-
foot, a domestic travesty and failure . . . on the escutcheon of the
great Bonaparte. The man who successfully conquered Europe, and built
new empires, failed at marriage. Napoleon divorced Josephine, and
the broken harp in Malmaison will ever stand as a mute monument
to love's failure and matrimonial disaster.[1]

In the 1920's, the broken harp, if ever, then indeed, sounded
with superlative irony a warning against the tragedy of a broken
home. An ever-increasing number of American marriages was ending in divorce. From 1910 to 1928 the annual ratio of divorces to
marriages rose alarmingly. In 1910 for every hundred marriages
there were 8.8 divorces; in 1920, 13.4; and in 1928, 16.5 or almost
one divorce for every six marriages.[2] The steady increase over an
extended period of time was due, apparently, to reasons other than
the war. The United States was without a peer in her number of
divorces, and much of the disgrace formerly accompanying divorce
suffered a marked decline.[3]

Few could deny the very obvious truth that the American home pattern was undergoing change. "The old-fashioned family home is rapidly disappearing."[4] "The American home life is in a state of chaos."[5] The American home may be changed but it is not vanishing[6] "Homes are being broken up in our country."[7]

Parental authority is waning. New sets of parents are needed; parents who have spunk enough to climb back upon the thrones in their own households which they have abdicated in favor of their children; parents who have energy enough to get their children out of bed in the morning early enough for them to wash their faces, comb their hair, and lace their shoes without the school's being obliged to give promotion credit for their doing so; parents who, when the shades of night begin to fall, look after their boys with the same degree of care that they give to their bull pup, which they chain up lest he associate with the strange cur on the street.[8]

How do religious groups specifically view divorce that is on the upward climb? Do they agree that it is threatening the institution of the home? Are they ready with solutions? For the answers to these, and other similar questions we will turn to our periodicals and listen to the comments of the editors and those for whom they write.

In the early months of the decade, the Southern Conference of Methodists, with an almost perceptible shudder, would remind Christian leaders to pause in their strenuous efforts to stem the tide of evils sweeping as a mighty flood over the social, economic, and ecclesiastical life of our country, and "summon all their powers of delineation, reproof, and persuasion to the task of checking the divorce evil which is undermining the very foundations of the home."[9]

The prime edifice of our Christian civilization is the home; when this is destroyed every fundamental institution of normal American life is endangered. Divorce, never so defiant and so flagrantly deadly as now, is a threat we must meet if we would maintain our Christian civilization.[10]

The group agrees with a certain Judge who has been deciding divorce cases over a period of years, that a divorce is no longer a stigma on a woman's name, but rather an asset.[11] The fate of our nation will inevitably be that of Greece and Rome unless the divorce evil is curbed.[12] For a nation that lets it go on is sure to die. How long will "the blessings of holy matrimony continue to give way to yelping passions?"[13]

The Methodists later in the period note that homes are being broken for unscriptural reasons, and this fact adds to the heinous evil of divorce. The great divergence of marriage and divorce legislation is worthy of the sober consideration of upright Christian citizens. A uniform marriage and divorce law, while not a complete answer to the current problem, would have an advantage in that all suits for annulment, separation, alimony, and divorce would be brought in the Federal Courts.[14]

The official position of the Methodist denomination is unmistakable in the statement of policy made in April, 1929.

. . . The Methodist Episcopal Church has not changed its law on the subject of divorce. It rather purposes to emphasize the importance of sustaining family life and of entirely avoiding divorce. The General Conference action and the statement of the Bishops call upon the ministers to adhere strictly to the rule of the Church in marrying a divorced person. The propriety in performing a ceremony for a divorced person is based not on the language of the petition at court, but upon the facts, and the facts must confirm the adulterous guilt of the former spouse of the now remarrying innocent one.[15]

In passing, it might be noted here that adultery was recognized by the group as the only cause for a divorce.

A little later, a certain perceptible shaft of light pierces the gloom and the group shakes off its melancholy and disconsolateness to bask in the golden glow of hope. That divorces are definitely too frequent, the Southern Conference admits and deplores. But it decides to look at the great number of marriages which are permanent. True, it would be desired that all unions might be permanent, but perfection in marriage is scarcely to be expected when every other feature of life has some failures. Our way of life has produced a high degree of nervousness, luxury, idleness, and whimsicality in both men and women. When the tests of marriage come upon these it is not surprising that many of them fail. This is not sufficient cause for unqualified alarm. "The home is going to stand."[16]

The Northern Conference looks upon the progressive increase in the number of divorces as "one of the most conspicuous signs of the decline of those homely virtues on which Anglo-Saxon society has rested."[17] The changed attitude of public opinion may possibly be due to the fact that "familiarity with the subject has dulled sensibility" or to the more liberal view that "the rising generation takes

... on the matrimonial relation."[18] The group quotes the disciplinary paragraph, "No divorce except for adultery shall be regarded by the Church as lawful,"[19] and would admonish all

> that the farther society departs from this rigid standard, the more it will relax the sanctity of marriage, the home, and the family. . . . When these institutions fall, civilization, as we know it, will fall with them.[20]

Presbyterians are concerned about American divorces in Paris. There is a foundation for their anxiety since the higher social class made Paris divorces fashionable. Law in the French capital was complaisant. For anyone unmindful of the cost of a little time and money, a Paris divorce was easily obtained. The standard causes stated were desertion, cruelty, and adultery, but much laxity was apparent in their interpretation.

> Desertion often meant a collusive arrangement whereby both parties had agreed to separate long enough to make divorce possible; cruelty was interpreted to cover "mental anguish" caused by any misconduct whatsoever on the party against whom complaint was laid; adultery was often a staged affair to satisfy the technicalities of the law.[21]

Against this background of fact, the Presbyterians lament that "the divorce mill is running at too rapid a rate in the French capital. Over two hundred American divorces were handed down last year."[22]

The American Hebrew, speaking for the Reform Jewish element, harshly calls to task those Rabbis who, "continue to give the rabbinical divorce before a civil divorce is granted."[23] These Rabbis ought to know that the rabbinical divorce is illegal before the civil processes have been complied with. There is not a trace of mercy in the plea the periodical makes for heavy fines and jail sentences to be meted to those who willfully or ignorantly issue illegal divorces.[24]

Having salved its conscience in regard to this legal technicality, the journal of the Reform Jews indulges in a satirical diatribe. Here, as often before, this periodical seems to stand apart both in attitude and in expression. It seems to be scoffing merrily at those who think a honeymoon can last a life time by periodic separations.

> The device of two establishments for people intent on following their own pursuits is not altogether new. The old ascetics inevitably fled the presence of woman whenever they wished their thoughts to soar heavenward. It will be recalled that St. Anthony tried it, not with

complete success, it is true, but with encouraging results. In this era of emancipated womanhood, the process is reversed. When a fair one wishes to woo the seven arts, she, too, must flee into the desert, (metaphorical, fortunately; here used as euphemism for comfy studio) and abjure the company of the opposite sex. In moments when our matrimonial barks of conventional design, sailing familiar, charted courses over troubled waters, run into storms or dreadful calms, it will be cheering to think of husband and wife in their twin motor boats hailing each other when they choose and following their own sweet wills when they don't.[25]

A little space is requested by the Episcopalians first to remind Christian people of the compelling need of something more than sighs over the sure destruction of family life by the increasingly rapid spread of divorce.[26] The Episcopalian Bishop of Kentucky is then presented as voicing, succinctly and well, what the Church has in mind.

> In the Church we have been faulted for standing for the sacredness of matrimony and for maintaining rigid divorce laws. We continue so to stand and to uphold these ideals as real promoters of the welfare of society and of the state. We cater to no applause and we covet no praise for liberality by lowering our standards to conform to the easy conscience which lightly reverences so sacred a thing as marriage. Make marriage holy matrimony. . . . [27]

Marriage is a legal contract, it is true, but it is vastly more. "It is a sacrament; and nothing whatever can undo what God has done there."[28]

There must be a certain degree of realism in facing the problem and in the case where a marriage is absolutely a failure, the remedy of separation *a mensa et thoro* may relieve the condition. "Between that and dissolution of the marriage bond there is a vast difference."[29]

Unitarian ranks are not found in this school of thought. The crux of this knotty problem of divorce lies in the indisputable fact that "the average men and women of thirty today are far apart from their fathers and mothers"[30] in their thinking on the subject. It is not to be denied that even "the lust of the flesh" is not so greatly condemned as it once was. These changed attitudes have come because "we are more philosophical . . . than we used to be."[31]

> We know the evil of sin as much as ever, but we spend less time in remarking about it than we did when our religious teaching consigned

sinners to hell and pushed them outside the pale as so many pariahs. Religion has toned down its austerities.[32]

Hence, the Unitarians are convinced that the majesty of God's law in the relation of marriage, or in any other relation, has not been renounced. Today people are less solemn and contemplative about it —therein lies the difference. We have become players in the

> great game of life. When some one cheats or foozles us, we note it but do not rack our souls about it. We buck up somewhat and play a little straighter ourselves. We take that marvelously sound position of the gospel of not being overcome by the evil, as the older lugubrious religious professionals were.[33]

With undisguised impatience this group aims sharp remarks against denominations which presume to pass on the religious validity of some marriages by placing themselves on record as saying "that certain marriages performed in accord with the laws of the United States of America are not valid in the eyes of Christians."[34] The question of marriage becomes for these churches not a matter of love between the contracting parties but one of technicalities. They lose themselves in points such as consent of the parties and consummation of the marriage.[35] Despite their irritation, the Unitarians would like to sympathize with the members of these churches, for whom there is no escape.

> If Jesus was God, his views on divorce must bind Christians for all time. Recognizing that in fact many marriages are hopeless, the theologians will do their best to find a loophole. But come out squarely . . . they cannot. The doctrine of the Incarnation has cut off the way of sense and humanitarianism here, as in too many other instances.[36]

Not at all would this denominational group sanction the relaxing of due regard and honor for the bonds of marriage. But the bonds must be those of careful love and mutual respect and not the iron manacles of law.[37] Such attitudes will not make for more divorce but for more indissoluble unions. The new way is the better way.

> The . . . older marriage idea consisted in this: The marriage having been divinely sanctioned in heaven, as the preacher said, both man and wife were relatively free to disregard their mutual obligation as they often did, each gradually falling away from, instead of cultivating the other, and the relationship becoming a dull matter of child-bearing,

livelihood, housekeeping, and a vegetative approach to hard and dry old age. That tragedy is written on the pages of our customs.[38] Lutherans are ready with a rebuttal. It is precisely the present day school of thought on morals that is doing much toward helping the divorce mill "to grind out its unhealthy grist with cheerless monotony."[39] It is seeking to encourage a disregard for the sacredness of the marriage bond and to engender false notions as to its meaning in the minds of youth.[40] The alarming increase in divorces is proofsecure that the so-called "modern philosophy" is paving the way for the complete destruction of the American home. With an urgency born of desperation, there are those of the "old school" who clamor for legislation. But "let us not deceive ourselves and expect too much of legislation."[41] Granting that laws concerning marriage and divorce are in need of revision, these Missouri Synod members, nevertheless, think that the mere forcing of people to live together in wedlock is not a satisfactory solution. They recall that, even in the Old Testament, divorce could not be entirely avoided and "God Himself instituted government and inspired its laws!"[42] The hardness of hearts then wrung permission from the Almighty. The same accusation may be leveled against the world now.[43]

The Word of God must soften hard hearts. That hammer of God "that breaketh the rock in pieces" must be used upon the hard hearts of men. This Word has transformed many a lion into a lamb and is as powerful today as it ever was.[44]

Zealously and enthusiastically, the denominational group presents what it considers an unfailing answer to the disunions Satan is instigating.

We Christians have the solution of the problem. "Faith cometh by hearing and hearing by the Word of God!" By the hearing of faith the Holy Spirit is given. And "the fruit of the Spirit is love, joy, peace, longsuffering, gentleness, goodness, faith, meekness, temperance!" And where these fruits are found, divorce and lawsuits do not find the soil very favorable.[45]

United Lutherans have ready but pungent words to express their sentiments on the same subject. "That society is degenerating because marriage is no longer held as a sacred contract goes without saying."[46] The hasty entrance into marriage by emotional and fickle people, the total lack of seriousness with which it is entered, the disgraceful levity with which wedlock is often spoken about and pictured in cartoons, the selfish unwillingness to face duties, responsibilities, and trials of marriage—all reveal a temper and state of mind and morals that make one tremble for the future.[47]

It is a duty incumbent on all to stand up to the evil of divorce. "No single evil in the country today is cutting a deeper gash into the vitals of the nation than it. It aims its dagger at the home."[48]

The indifference and supineness of society allow this crime to run riot. The fine sense of moral perception must be recovered if this tide of evil is to be stemmed. It is time society realized the unvarnished truth that the divorce evil is incriminatingly symptomatic of a disease that lies deeper.[49]

> That disease is immorality—and a kind of immorality that has been reduced to a science. Under the guise of an outer show of respectability, married men and women play fast and loose with all that gives wedded life its ethical significance and charm and beauty. Darwin shocked the world when he traced the descent of man down to the ape. His theory is still in need of proof; but if anything could induce us to believe the theory, it would be the orgy of animalism among a class of well-fed and well-groomed polygamists whose ethics is the ethics of the jungle—only vastly more reprehensible in the sight of God and man.[50]

Like their fellow Lutherans, this group also has a remedy to propose for the cure of the rampant abuse.

> There is only one way of solving the divorce problem. It is to get the Christian home to function as it should, to train the young in the fear of the Lord, which is the beginning of wisdom.[51]

The Watchman-Examiner prefaces what it has to say with a phrase—laconic, but emphatic in its brevity. "We do not believe in easy divorces. Unfaithfulness to the marriage vow is the only Scriptural ground for divorce."[52]

Although recognizing grounds for divorce under specific conditions, the Baptists, for whom the periodical is expressive, frown with deep-seated revulsion on the all-time high record of the United States. In 1921, "every four minutes of every hour of every day and night, some American couple arranges separation."[53]

But just because divorce has become the most hideously common thing, the official organ of Northern Baptists would insist, it is not by that token to be sanctioned. Formerly divorce startled people. Such days are no more.

The breaking of marriage vows is one of the things which people have first abhorred and then embraced. It can hardly be said, as it was in Rome, that there are women who number their years by their husbands. But there are some who have made an admirable beginning.[54]

This group is in perfect accord with their fellow Baptists and grant that separations and divorces may sometimes be necessary. In Scripture, at least, one cause for divorce is recognized.[55]

But we do say strongly that in order to preserve the integrity of the home, which occupies an important place in God's plan for men, our churches must take a serious view of divorce. Marriage is a sacred thing, the family is a holy institution, and no Christian should take a light and flippant view of either, or share the prevalent looseness of thought regarding them.[56]

The Catholics have pen in hand eager to command our attention. To the expressions of opinion from this group we now turn our glance.

Uneasily does the mind of *The Commonweal* rest in the unhappy distinction of the country's registering more divorces than any other civilized nation. It muses aloud regarding some items behind the startling divorce figures.[57]

The material we send to the marriage altar has degenerated; indeed, the altar itself has been pretty generally discarded. If there are to be good brides and good grooms, there must be behind them good fathers and good mothers; and our supply of these precious social assets is rapidly diminishing. When all are gone, we shall need only to open more divorce courts.[58]

But perhaps, as fundamental as these are, the *America* interrupts, they may still be considered but facades of the divorce evil—the foundations are deeper. "When the sundering of the marriage bond is sanctioned for any cause whatever except death, we unloose a flood that no man can control."[59] One cause only was recognized as grounds for divorce a hundred years ago. At least fifty-two causes are recognized now as legal, while bad faith and chicanery multiply even these.[60] There is much that the State can, and, in fact, must do to defend the indissolubility of the matrimonial contract, but the strongest defense of an inviolable marriage bond is a generation trained in morality and religion.

These Catholics who speak through the *America* would urge various religious denominations to exercise a concerted inflexibility as a united front against the flagrant evil.

In crisp, pithy terms the journal goes on to delineate the position of the Catholic Church.

> The Church . . . never grants a divorce, that is, she never dissolves a valid marriage, ratified and consummated, leaving the parties free to enter into a new matrimonial contract. She can, however, declare that a reputed marriage has been null and void.[61]

Now that the journal has traced out this premise, it is ready to comment still further on the problem. It believes the stability of family life in the United States is in the balance. The ideal of monogamy is being replaced by state and ecclesiastical tolerance of polygamy. As long as divorce and remarriage are licensed, the evil cannot be smitten at the root.[62] When the dissolution of a true marriage is permitted, human ingenuity will not fail to find reasons for divorce.[63]

The number of those who have come forward with plans to check this national scandal has been legion. Suggestions have ranged from the enforced teaching of parenthood in the home to a constitutional amendment, giving the Federal Government the right to legislate for marriage and its dissolution. Between these two extremes, have been schemes and proposals of varying degrees of sense and absurdity.[64] However, this welter of disorganized activity has a redeeming factor in that it indicates a common recognition that divorce is an evil for which a remedy must be found.

These Catholics would remind the would-be-reformers that divorce may not be treated as though it were purely a matter of economics or of social policy.[65] "Primarily it is a moral question and it can never be solved satisfactorily on other than moral grounds."[66]

The *America* admits that grounds which justify a separation *a mensa et thoro* can exist, and can be accepted as valid by competent authority in Church and State. A separation of this nature, of course, keeps the bond intact and forbids new nuptials.[67]

A piece of homely advice the group wishes to pass on—advice which, if lived out, would go a far way to lay this Banquo's ghost of divorce.

Marriage is give and take. Husband and wife cannot promise to retain forever the first fine raptures of youthful love but they can vow fidelity and keep their vow.[68]

Of the triple assault on the home pattern, divorce, it would seem, from the rather profuse comments, appeared to be the most menacing in the thoughts and opinions of the religious leaders and spokesmen. The question as to whether moral standards as they pertained to matrimony were improving or degenerating was widely but perhaps inconclusively debated. But that transitions from older views to newer ones on the American home were in progress, no one could deny. And transitions are seldom painless!

"Upon the loom of thought
We weave our fancies."

—T. B. Aldrich, *Cloth of Gold.*

CHAPTER XIII

Concluding Comments

The loom of thought has woven the tapestry of opinion of life in the 1920's. In the preceding ten chapters, we have followed the tangled skein of changing manners and morals in their fashioning the fabric of attitudes during the third decade of the twentieth century. And into the weaving of the pattern have gone the warp and woof of contrary and, ofttimes, conflicting sentiments. The design, at intervals, may have seemed to lose its pattern as one or other publication dropped a thread, as it were, by maintaining silence on an issue. And if the reverse side of the tapestry presented but a maze of ill-matched shades in a profusion of knots during those years, by the end of the decade the design had been traced clearly and unmistakably. This tapestry of opinion, it has been seen, was interlaced with threads, both golden, with joyful hope for the future, and somber, with grim forebodings for the coming age. But the various shades of attitudes and different blends of sentiment have only enhanced the study.

And now, as we stand back and look at the finished work, a few concluding comments seem timely and in order.

As we have made our way through the preceding ten chapters, a panorama, a cross section, of life in the Twenties was unfolded. In viewing this gamut of life, from the literature going into the American home to the sundering of the home itself by divorce, these chapters have shown that manners and morals were no longer being channeled in traditional streams. These pages have, likewise, proved that the religious editors and spokesmen were keenly alerted to the shiftings in the contemporary scene, and in their journals have reconstructed for future generations a picture of their day. Periodical literature thus has no mean role in the sphere of historical research. As a source, it has validity. Combined with other sources at the command of the historian, it is a definite aid in the task of rebuilding the buried past.

Examining the weaving a little more intently, it will be noted that many threads of thought strung along the frame of agreement have met other threads of thought strung contrariwise to these—thus providing the indispensible warp and woof in any fabric.

As regards the home pattern, all the periodicals expressed themselves in the rebel camp in the matter of companionate marriage, with the exception of the Unitarians who would seem to view it as an old actuality wearing a new label, and of Northern Baptists who are inclined to dismiss the problem as a usual "tempest in a teapot" phenomenon. The Reform Jewish element, both here and in the discussion on birth control, is noncommittal, whereas Lutherans, Catholics, Baptists, and Presbyterians have evinced decided and determined opposition to contraception. Unitarians, Methodists, and Episcopalians afford it a grudging tolerance or a sanctioned approval.

Divorce marshals to its ranks no crusading proponents directly, but at the same time, it does not lack some ardent sympathizers. *The American Hebrew,* while not unfurling its banner unequivocally, objects to rabbinical divorce before a legal divorce has been granted— on this latter type there is, apparently, an intended taciturnity. Unitarians hold that marriage bonds should be forged by love and not by "iron manacles of law," thereby disagreeing vehemently with the other denominations.

The agreeing and conflicting threads of sentiment follow in somewhat the same sequence in the field of the motion picture, where the immoral aspect of the films is predominantly distressing to the majority of editors. Unitarians and Jews are aligned against censorship and Catholics seem inclined to weave their way between either extreme.

In fashions, too, is there a similar pattern with this one change: Catholic groups have moved from the center to enter their protest with the others who decry immodest styles. This same theme works itself as a motif throughout the designing of the entire pattern— cosmetics, smoking, and the like—with Unitarians and Jews usually bearing the banner of the opposition against the other denominations. Grouped with the reformers, however, will these two segments be in condemning the ever-increasing professionalism in sports.

One finds an evenness of stitch as the shuttle of thought weaves opinion pertinent to the place of the automobile in the life of the generation. Every editor, voicing the sentiments of his constituents, sees the tremendous strides the automotive industry has made and concomitantly the benefits that accrue to the citizenry therefrom. Each spokesman, likewise, is convinced that the automobile has not come as an unmixed blessing: the toll of human lives sacrificed to its speed, the furthering of crime, the inducement to youthful escapades must be charged against it.

Unmindful of individual threads again to better appraise the completed tapestry, one may say that to all the editors, the Twenties presented a period of liberation of the human spirit, but for the majority of them that spirit seemed to be liberated in a maelstrom of worshippers of the body, of champions of speed, of adventurers in the ephemeral, of creators of the imaginative movie-world.

The Twenties had, indeed, been a decade of unbounded exuberance, but by the time the era ended it seems to have spent its enthusiasm. The next years, with new and poignant problems, were already creeping in to divert attention and interest. New problems would mean a new pattern of public opinion.

The loom of thought was once again at its task!

Appendices

APPENDIX A

ESTIMATED POPULATION OF UNITED STATES[1]

1920	106,418,284
1921	107,833,284
1922	109,248,393
1923	110,663,502
1924	112,078,611
1925	115,378,094
1926	117,135,817
1927	118,628,000
1928	120,501,000
1929	121,770,000

MEMBERSHIP OF RELIGIOUS DENOMINATIONS IN THE UNITED STATES[2]

	1926	*1916*
Baptists	8,246,266	7,153,313
Episcopalians	1,859,086	1,092,821
Jewish	4,081,242	357,135[3]
Lutherans	3,939,108	2,467,516
Methodists	8,033,957	7,166,451
Presbyterians	2,623,026	2,255,626
Roman Catholics	18,605,003	15,721,815
Unitarians	60,152	82,515

171

MARRIAGES IN THE UNITED STATES[4]

Year	Number	Rate
1916	1,675,775	10.6
1917	1,144,200	11.1
1918	1,000,109	9.7
1919	1,150,186	11.0
1920	1,274,476	12.0
1921	1,163,863	10.7
1922	1,134,151	10.3
1923	1,229,784	11.0
1924	1,184,574	10.4
1925	1,188,334	10.3
1926	1,202,574	10.2
1927	1,201,053	10.1
1928	1,182,497	9.8
1929	1,232,559	10.1

Rates per 1,000 estimated midyear population.

BIRTHS IN THE UNITED STATES[5]

Year	Number	Rate
1916	818,983	25.0
1917	1,353,792	24.7
1918	1,363,649	24.6
1919	1,373,438	22.3
1920	1,508,874	23.7
1921	1,714,261	24.2
1922	1,774,911	22.3
1923	1,792,646	22.2
1924	1,930,614	22.4
1925	1,878,880	21.5
1926	1,856,068	20.7
1927	2,137,836	20.6
1928	2,233,149	19.8
1929	2,169,920	18.9

Rates in the above table are per 1,000 population.

DIVORCES IN THE UNITED STATES[6]

Year	Number	Rate
1916	114,000	1.1
1917	121,564	1.2
1918	116,254	1.1
1919	141,527	1.3
1920	170,505	1.6
1921	159,580	1.5
1922	148,815	1.4
1923	165,096	1.5
1924	170,952	1.5
1925	175,449	1.5
1926	184,678	1.6
1927	196,292	1.6
1928	200,176	1.7
1929	205,876	1.7

Rates per 1,000 estimated midyear population.

APPENDIX B

The following are excerpts from letters testifying as to the position of the various religious periodicals examined in this study in the respective denominations.

"I am happy to concur in stating that both *America* and *The Commonweal* are very representative Catholic publications."

MOST REVEREND JOSEPH E. RITTER
Archbishop of Saint Louis

Office of the Archbishop
3810 Lindell Boulevard
Saint Louis, Missouri

———

"There is no paper that is an official organ of the entire denomination for the period of the 1920's. *The Watchman-Examiner* has held a place of influence, however, dating back beyond that period. It has always represented what might be termed in the best sense of the word, a "conservative approach" to all questions. In the period you designate, it represented much more of the general Baptist mind than may be said for the period since 1930.

"*The Baptist* reflects more specifically the views of the Northern Baptist Convention, which is now known as the American Baptist Convention as a result of the action taken in Boston in 1950 to that effect."

EDWARD B. WILLINGHAM

National Baptist Memorial Church
Sixteenth Street and Columbia Road, N.W.
Washington 9, D. C.

———

"We do have files of *The Word and Way*, the official publication of the Missouri Baptist Association."

T. W. MEDEARIS, *Superintendent General*

Missouri Baptist Building
Jefferson City, Missouri

———

"*The Christian Advocate* is the only publication with all the Methodists. It is as official as we have any paper."

CHARLES W. FLINT, *Bishop of Washington*

The Methodist Church
100 Maryland Avenue, N.E.
Washington 2, D. C.

"In 1939 unification brought together the Methodist Episcopal Church, the Methodist Episcopal Church South, and the Methodist Protestant Church. There was a Christian Advocate representing the whole Church before 1940. Then this paper was formed from the merger of seven papers. *The Christian Advocate*, published in Nashville, was recognized as representing the Methodist Episcopal Church South, while *The Christian Advocate*, published in New York, may be considered as presenting views of the Methodist Episcopal Church."

T. OTTO NOLL, *Editor*

Christian Advocate
740 Rush Street
Chicago 11, Illinois

"*The Lutheran Witness* is an official, bi-weekly publication of the Missouri Synod."

DR. P. BRETSCHER, *Acting President*

Concordia Theological Seminary
801 De Mun
Saint Louis, Missouri

"*The Lutheran* is the official news magazine of the United Lutheran Church and would correctly reflect our point of view."

OSCAR W. BLACKWELDER

Lutheran Church of the Reformation
212 East Capitol Street
Washington 2, D. C.

"*The Presbyterian Magazine* from 1919 to 1926 was the official magazine of the Presbyterian Church, U. S. A."

CHARLES A. ANDERSON, *Librarian*

Presbyterian Historical Society
Witherspoon Building
Philadelphia 7, Pennsylvania

"*The Living Church* is widely read in the Episcopal Church and would be generally representative in the area of manners and morals. It would represent what is commonly known among us as "high church" or "catholic" position.

RT. REV. ANGUS DUN, *Bishop of Washington*

Diocese of Washington
1702 Rhode Island Avenue, N.W.
Washington 6. D. C.

"In the nineteen twenties, *The Christian Register* was an independent Unitarian publication, quite free of denominational control. The basic fact is, of course, that the Unitarian churches are founded on individual freedom of belief, and this freedom reflects itself in all phases of denominational life, including *The Christian Register*.

A. POWELL DAVIES

All Souls' Church
Sixteenth and Harvard Streets
Washington 9, D. C.

"*The American Hebrew* is a Jewish publication worth perusing. It does reflect a good deal of the trends and the currents of the times."

DAVID H. PANITZ, *Rabbi*

Adas Israel Congregation
Connecticut Avenue at Porter Street, N.W.
Washington 8, D. C.

List of References

CHAPTER I

1. Lucy Salmon, *The Newspaper and the Historian* (New York: Oxford University Press, 1923), p. 491.
2. The denominational groups represented in this work were decided upon after consulting the figures of the Religious Census of 1916. They were:

Catholics	33%
Protestants	55%

Baptists	19%
Methodists	18%
Lutherans	7%
Presbyterians	6%
Episcopalians	3%
Unitarians	2%

This accounted for approximately 88% of the Christian population; the remaining 12% was divided into small fractional units of multiple off-shoots of one or other of the above. The 12% unrepresented in this study does not have individual publications. Jewish opinion as reflected in the periodicals of the Reform group is also included in the examination.
3. Cf., Appendix, pp. 174-176 for statements from qualified spokesmen among Catholics, Protestants, and Jews.

CHAPTER II

1. Cf. *The Lutheran*, XI (December 27, 1928), 3.
   Cf. *Ibid.*, X (June 21, 1928), 3.
   Cf. *Ibid.*, X (June 14, 1928), 3.
   Cf. *The Watchman-Examiner*, IX² (August 4, 1921), 973.
2. Cf. *The Baptist*, I¹ (January 31, 1920), 8.
3. *Ibid.*, IV (May 12, 1923), 455.
4. *Ibid.*, III (July 1, 1922), 681-682.
5. *The Watchman-Examiner*, X¹ (June 22, 1922), 773. Also cf. *Canadian Baptist*, IX (July 13, 1920), 123. Similar observation is also made by *The Lutheran*, II (August 12, 1920), 242.
6. *The Baptist*, II (July 16, 1921), 750.
7. *The Watchman-Examiner*, XII² (July 24, 1924), 949.
8. *Ibid.*, IX² (July 14, 1921), 871.
9. *The Lutheran*, II (August 12, 1920), 242.
10. *The Commonweal*, V (November 10, 1926), 2.
11. *The Christian Register*, CIII (November 27, 1924), 1139.

12. *The Commonweal*, I (February 18, 1925), 395.
13. *Ibid.*, I (May 6, 1925), 697.
14. *Ibid.*, I (April 29, 1925), 670.
15. *The Living Church*, LXXIX (May 19, 1928), 77.
16. *Ibid.*, LXXVIII (March 17, 1928), 661.
17. *The Christian Register*, CVII (January 19, 1928), 42-43.
18. *The Baptist*, VIII[1] (April 16, 1927), 503. Cf. also *Ibid.*, IX[1] (April 28, 1928), 527, and *Ibid.*, X[2] (October 12, 1929), 1290.
19. *The Christian Advocate*, N. Y., CII (April 21, 1927), 485. Cf. also *Ibid.*, C (January 15, 1925), 71.
20. *The Lutheran*, X (March 15, 1928), 3. Cf. also *Ibid.*, IX (April 21, 1927), 4, and *Ibid.*, X (June 28, 1928), 3.
21. *America*, XXXVIII (December 31, 1927), 286.
22. *The Watchman-Examiner*, XII[1] (June 5, 1924), 707. Cf. also *Ibid.*, IX[1] (May 5, 1921), 548.
23. *Lutheran Witness*, XLIII (May 20, 1924), 199. Cf. also *Ibid.*, XLII (February 13, 1923), 53.
24. *Ibid.*, XL (June 7, 1921), 185.
25. *The Christian Advocate*, N. Y., C (November 26, 1925), 1445. Cf. also *Ibid.*, CIV (January 17, 1929), 69, and *Ibid.*, XCVI (January 20, 1921), 67.
26. *The Living Church*, LXIV (February 26, 1921), 524.
27. *The Christian Advocate*, N. Y., CIV (January 17, 1929), 69. Cf. also *Ibid.*, XCV[2] (October 28, 1920), 1426.
28. *Ibid.*, XCV[2] (July 15, 1920), 948.
29. *The Lutheran*, IX (July 7, 1927), 3. Also *Ibid.*, X (July 26, 1928), 4, *Ibid.*, IV (August 31, 1922), 3, *Ibid.*, III (December 23, 1920), 4, and *Ibid.*, XII (October 10, 1929), 4. *The Christian Register*, CVI (February 10, 1927), 106, speaks in a similar tenor.
30. *The Living Church*, LXIX (May 19, 1923), 76.
31. Cf. *The Lutheran*, X (February 2, 1928), 4, and *The Christian Register*, CV (October 7, 1926), 903.
32. *The Commonweal*, VII (November 30, 1927), 746.
33. *The Christian Advocate*, N. Y., CIII (December 6, 1928), 1493.
34. *The American Hebrew*, CXIV (January 4, 1924), 233.
35. *The Commonweal*, XI (December 11, 1929), 157.
36. *New Palestine*, III (August 11, 1922), 97.
37. *Ibid.*, III (July 14, 1922), 34.
38. Cf. *The Lutheran*, IV (January 5, 1922), 16, and *Ibid.*, X (September 6, 1928), 12.
39. *Ibid.*, II (May 20, 1920), 34.
40. *The Baptist*, III (February 24, 1922), 73.
41. *The Watchman-Examiner*, XI[2] (August 9, 1923), 1007.
42. *The Christian Register*, CVI (June 30, 1927), 580.
43. Cf. *Lutheran Witness*, XLII (June 5, 1923), 178.
44. *Ibid.*, XXXIX (January 6, 1920), 5.
45. *The Christian Advocate*, N. Y., C (October 15, 1925), 1254. Cf. also *Ibid.*, XCVIII (May 24, 1923), 646, *Ibid.*, C (April 30, 1925), 549, and *Ibid.*, CI (January 14, 1926), 38. In the following citations, *The Christian Advocate* will indicate the journal printed in Nashville, Tennessee, the official organ of the Southern group of Methodists. *The Christian Advocate*, N. Y., will signify the publication of Methodists of the Northern Conference. It might be noted here that in 1939 a union between the two sections was realized.

46. *Ibid.*, C (April 30, 1925), 549. Cf. *The Christian Advocate*, LXXXIV (June 15, 1923), 755.
47. *The Lutheran*, I (February 26, 1920), 872.
48. *The Christian Advocate*, N. Y., C (September 10, 1925), 1091.
49. Cf. *Ibid.*, XCVI (January 13, 1921), 34.
50. *The Watchman-Examiner*, XII[1] (March 13, 1924), 327.
51. *Ibid.*, XIV[1] (May 27, 1926), 644.
52. *The Lutheran*, XI (September 5, 1929), 15.
53. *The Presbyterian Magazine*, XXX (January, 1924), 28.
54. *Ibid.*, p. 28.
55. *Ibid.*, XXVII (March, 1922), 510.
56. *The Christian Register*, CV (February 16, 1926), 1131.
57. *The Watchman-Examiner*, XVII[2] (July 18, 1929), 898.
58. *The Christian Register*, CIII (January 31, 1924), 107.
59. *Ibid.*, CIV (February 26, 1925), 195.
60. *The Watchman-Examiner*, X[1] (March 9, 1922), 295. For similar comments cf. *Ibid.*, XII[1] (February 28, 1924), 261, and *Ibid.*, XV[1] (December 1, 1927), 1511. Also *The Christian Advocate*, N. Y., C (June 25, 1925), 805, and *The Living Church*, LXXIV (April 24, 1926), 855, and *America*, XXXIV (January 23, 1926), 343.

CHAPTER III

1. Mark Sullivan, *Our Times* (New York: Charles Scribner's Sons, 1935), VI, 578-579.

CHAPTER IV

1. *The American Hebrew*, CXVIII (January 15, 1926), 321.
2. *The Lutheran*, II (May 20, 1920), 40.
3. *Lutheran Witness*, XLVI (December 27, 1927), 452.
4. *The Lutheran*, VIII (May 6, 1926), 14.
5. *Ibid.*, p. 14.
6. *Lutheran Witness*, XXXIX (March 16, 1920), 88.
7. *The Lutheran*, VI (March 27, 1924), 15.
8. *Lutheran Witness*, XXXIX (December 7, 1920), 391.
9. *The Lutheran*, VIII (May 6, 1926), 14.
10. *Ibid.*, II (May 20, 1920), 40.
11. *Lutheran Witness*, XLVI (December 27, 1927), 452.
12. *The Lutheran*, II (May 20, 1920), 40.
13. *Ibid.*, IX (September 15, 1927), 15.
14. Cf. *The Christian Register*, CIV (August 27, 1925), 835.
15. *Ibid.*, p. 835.
16. *Ibid.*, CV (May 27, 1926), 487.
17. *Ibid.*, C (February 24, 1921), 171.
18. *Ibid.*, p. 171.
19. *Ibid.*, p. 171.
20. *Ibid.*, CV (September 23, 1926), 858.
21. *Ibid.*, p. 858.
22. *Ibid.*, C (May 19, 1921), 459.
23. *The Commonweal*, V (February 16, 1927), 398.
24. *Ibid.*, III (April 14, 1926), 621.
25. *America*, XXXI (September 13, 1924), 513.

26. *Ibid.,* XXXI (September 27, 1924), 571.
27. *Ibid.,* p. 571.
28. *Ibid.,* p. 571.
29. *Ibid.,* p. 571.
30. *Ibid.,* XXXVI (November 13, 1926), 103.
31. *Ibid.,* p. 103.
32. *The Presbyterian Magazine,* XXXI (February, 1925), 61.
33. *Ibid.,* XXIX (February, 1923), 69.
34. *New Era Magazine,* XXVI (June, 1920), 407.
35. *The Presbyterian Magazine,* XXIX (August, 1923), 435.
36. *Ibid.,* p. 435.
37. *Ibid.,* XXXI (February, 1925), 61.
38. *The Presbyterian Banner,* CXII (November 26, 1925), 3.
39. *Ibid.,* p. 3.
40. *Ibid.,* p. 3.
41. *The Living Church,* LXXVII (August 20, 1927), 531.
42. *Ibid.,* p. 531.
43. *The Christian Advocate,* LXXXVIII (December 16, 1927), 1572. Cf.
    also *Ibid.,* LXXXI (November 5, 1920), 1429.
44. *Ibid.,* p. 1429.
45. *Ibid.,* LXXXIV (June 22, 1923), 788.
46. *Ibid.,* LXXXVIII (December 16, 1927), 1572.
47. *The Christian Advocate,* N. Y., CI (April 15, 1926), 454.
48. *The Baptist,* II (March 26, 1921), 229.
49. Cf. *Ibid.,* III (November 11, 1922), 1266.
50. Cf. *Ibid.,* III (August 19, 1922), 883.
51. *The Word and Way,* LXIII (May 12, 1927), 2.
52. Cf. *Ibid.,* p. 2.
53. *The Watchman-Examiner,* VIII² (July 29, 1920), 951.

CHAPTER V

1. Cf. *Facts and Figures of the Automobile Industry* (New York: National
   Automobile Chamber of Commerce, 1931 ed.), pp. 3, 16.
2. From a parody published in *Life* and quoted by Foster Rhea Dulles,
   Twentieth Century America (Boston: Houghton Mifflin Company, 1945),
   p. 55.
3. Cf. Ralph C. Epstein, *The Automobile Industry* (Chicago: 1928), pp. 4, 6.
4. For a specialized treatment of the industry, the following works are to
   be recommended: David L. Cohn, *Combustion on Wheels: An Informal
   History of the Automobile Age* (Boston: Houghton and Mifflin Company,
   1944).
   Lawrence H. Seltzer, *A Financial History of the American Automobile
   Industry* (Boston: Houghton and Mifflin Company, 1928).
   More general information may be had from works such as George Soule,
   Prosperity Decade (New York: Rinehart and Co., Inc., 1947).
   James Truslow Adams, *Our Business Civilization* (New York: Albert and
   Charles Boni, 1929).
5. Perhaps Chapter VIII, "The Saga of the Motor Car," in Preston William
   Slosson, *The Great Crusade and After* (New York: Macmillan and Co.,
   1930), pp. 219-250, presents as adequate a summary of social effects of
   the automobile as might be drawn up. There is nothing unique or startling

in Professor Slosson's conclusion; rather it is his ability, in a telling terseness, to crystallize what other authors have observed or written that so admirably serves the purpose.

6. *The Baptist,* X[1] (March 9, 1929), 312.
7. *Ibid.,* I[2] (October 23, 1920), 1320.
8. *Ibid.,* p. 1320.
9. *Ibid.,* I[1] (February 21, 1920), 116.
10. *Ibid.,* I[2] (October 23, 1920), 1320.
11. *Ibid.,* p. 1320.
12. *Ibid.,* p. 1320.
13. *Ibid.,* p. 1320.
14. *Ibid.,* I[1] (February 21, 1920), 116.
15. *The Watchman-Examiner,* X[1] (April 27, 1922), 519.
16. *Ibid.,* p. 519.
17. *Ibid.,* XIV[1] (April 15, 1926), 455.
18. *Ibid.,* XIII[2] (November 12, 1925), 1453.
19. *Ibid.,* XVII[1] (January 10, 1929), 41.
20. *The Baptist,* I[2] (August 7, 1920), 965.
21. *The Watchman-Examiner,* XII[2] (August 14, 1924), 1047.
22. *The Baptist,* I[2] (August 7, 1920), 965.
23. *Ibid.,* p. 965.
24. *The American Hebrew,* CXI (November 10, 1922), 685.
25. *The Living Church,* LXXIII (July 18, 1925), 385.
26. *Ibid.,* p. 385.
27. *America,* XXXV (July 10, 1926), 294.
28. Cf. *The Commonweal,* II (August 12, 1925), 320.
29. *America,* XXXII (October 18, 1924), 15.
30. Cf. *The Commonweal,* II (August 12, 1925), 320.
31. *America,* XXXII (October 18, 1924), 15.
32. *Ibid.,* XXXVII (August 20, 1927), 447.
33. *Ibid.,* p. 447.
34. *The Lutheran,* IX (September 22, 1927), 14.
35. *Ibid.,* p. 14.
36. *Ibid.,* p. 14.
37. *Lutheran Witness,* XLIII (August 12, 1924), 301.
38. *Ibid.,* p. 301.
39. *The Christian Advocate,* LXXXII (February 18, 1921), 195.
40. *Ibid.,* p. 195.
41. *Ibid.,* LXXXVIII (June 10, 1927), 708.
42. *Ibid.,* p. 708.
43. *Ibid.,* LXXXI (December 17, 1920), 1603.
44. *Ibid.,* LXXXIII (June 9, 1922), 707.
45. *Ibid.,* LXXXIII (December 1, 1922), 1508.
46. *Ibid.,* LXXXIV (May 4, 1923), 565.
47. *Ibid.,* p. 565.
48. *The Christian Register,* CVII (August 31, 1928), 691.
49. *Ibid.,* p. 691.
50. Cf. *The Christian Register,* CIV (April 9, 1925), 339.
51. *Ibid.,* CIII (August 28, 1924), 823.
52. *Ibid.,* p. 823.
53. *Ibid.,* C (October 13, 1921), 963.
54. *Ibid.,* p. 963.
55. Cf. *The Presbyterian Banner,* CIX (August 24, 1922), 1743.

56. *The Watchman-Examiner*, XIV[1] (February 11, 1926), 168.
57. *Ibid.*, p. 168.
58. *Ibid.*, p. 168.
59. *Ibid.*, p. 168.
60. *The Lutheran*, VI (July 24, 1924), 15.
61. *Ibid.*, XII (November 7, 1929), 3.
62. *The Living Church*, LXIV (November 6, 1920), 5.
63. *Ibid.*, LXXI (October 4, 1924), 719.
64. *The Commonweal*, II (July 1, 1925), 202.
65. *Ibid.*, p. 202.
66. Cf. W. S. Hiat, "Billions—Just for Fun," *Collier's*, LXXIV (October 25, 1924), 31.
67. *The Christian Register*, XCIX (October 7, 1920), 975.
68. *Ibid.*, p. 975.
69. Cf. *Ibid.*, CIV (October 22, 1925), 1026.
70. *Ibid.*, p. 1026.
71. Cf. *Ibid.*, p. 1026.
72. *The Presbyterian Banner*, CVIII (September 1, 1921), 283.
73. Cf. *Ibid.*, p. 283.
74. *Ibid.*, p. 283.
75. *Ibid.*, CXIII (January 20, 1927), 9.
76. *The Commonweal*, II (October 21, 1925), 579.
77. *Lutheran Witness*, XLV (October 19, 1926), 346.
78. *Ibid.*, p. 346.
79. *Ibid.*, p. 346.
80. *The Baptist*, V (October 18, 1924), 902.
81. *Ibid.*, III (March 4, 1922), 134.
82. *The Christian Advocate*, LXXXI (November 5, 1920), 1411.
83. *Ibid.*, p. 1411.
84. Cf. G. Rice, "The Real All-American," *Collier's*, LXXVIII (November 20, 1926), 16.
85. Cf. *Literary Digest*, LXXXIX (May 15, 1926), 31.
86. *America*, XXXV (October 2, 1926), 591.
87. *The Commonweal*, V (November 17, 1926), 36.
88. *America*, XXXIV (January 16, 1926), 320.
89. Cf. *Ibid.*, p. 320.
90. *Ibid.*, p. 320.
91. Cf. *The Christian Advocate*, LXXXV (October 10, 1924), 1283.
92. *Ibid.*, LXXXVI (May 1, 1925), 645.
93. *Ibid.*, LXXXIV (August 3, 1923), 981.
94. *The Christian Register*, CI (April 20, 1922), 367.
95. Cf. *America*, XXXV (October 2, 1926), 591.
96. *The Presbyterian Banner*, CXII (May 27, 1926), 6.
97. P. W. Slosson, *op. cit.*, p. 275.
98. *The Presbyterian Banner*, CVIII (July 7, 1921), 91.
99. *Ibid.*, p. 91.
100. *Ibid.*, CXIV (September 26, 1927), 11.
101. *Ibid.*, p. 11.
102. *Ibid.*, p. 11.
103. *The Baptist*, I[2] (December 11, 1920), 1577.
104. *The Watchman-Examiner*, XIII[1] (January 15, 1925), 71.
105. *Ibid.*, XIV[2] (September 23, 1926), 1191.
106. *Ibid.*, p. 1191.

107. *Ibid.*, XVII[1] (March 14, 1929), 329.
108. *The Christian Advocate*, N. Y., XCVI (January 27, 1921), 99, 100.
109. *Ibid.*, CI (August 26, 1926), 1020.
110. *Lutheran Witness*, XLV (October 19, 1926), 346.
111. *The Lutheran*, III (July 28, 1921), 17.
112. Cf. *Ibid.*, p. 17.
113. *Ibid.*, V (September 20, 1923), 15.
114. Cf. *The Watchman-Examiner*, X[1] (May 11, 1922), 583. Also *Ibid.*, XIII[1] (June 18, 1925), 783. Also *The Presbyterian Banner*, CVIII (June 16, 1921), 1.
115. *The Lutheran*, IV (January 26, 1922), 16, 17.
116. *Ibid.*, p. 17.
117. *The Living Church*, LXIV (January 1, 1921), 280.
118. Cf. *Ibid.*, LXV (June 11, 1921), 170.
119. Cf. *Ibid.*, p. 170.
120. Cf. *Ibid.*, LXIII (July 24, 1920), p. 427.
121. *Ibid.*, LXIII (August 21, 1920), 555.
122. Cf. *Ibid.*, p. 555.
123. *The American Hebrew*, CVI (April 9, 1920), 694.
124. *The Baptist*, VIII[2] (July 23, 1927), 955.
125. *Ibid.*, p. 955.
126. Quoted in *The Christian Advocate*, LXXXI (August 27, 1920), 1093.
127. *Ibid.*, LXXXIII (July 28, 1922), 931.
128. *Ibid.*, LXXXIII (September 22, 1922), 1187.
129. *Ibid.*, p. 1187.
130. *The Watchman-Examiner*, XVII[2] (August 22, 1929), 1065.
131. *The Presbyterian Banner*, CXIV (October 20, 1927), 9.
132. Cf. *Ibid.*, p. 9.
133. *The Lutheran*, VI (October 11, 1923), 17.
134. Cf. *Ibid.*, VIII (October 15, 1925), 15.
135. *The Presbyterian Banner*, CXIII (September 2, 1926), 9.
136. *Ibid.*, p. 9.
137. *Lutheran Witness*, XLII (May 22, 1923), 170.
138. *Ibid.*, p. 170.
139. *The Christian Register*, CII (April 26, 1923), 387.
140. *The Watchman-Examiner*, XV[1] (May 5, 1927), 551.
141. *Ibid.*, p. 551.
142. *The Lutheran*, VIII (September 16, 1926), 13.

CHAPTER VI

1. *Eccl.* 3, 4.
2. *New York Times*, March 13, 1927.
3. *The Commonweal*, IV (October 6, 1926), 516.
4. *Lutheran Witness*, XL (January 4, 1921), 9.
5. *Ibid.*, p. 9.
6. *Ibid.*, XXXIX (August 31, 1920), 279.
7. *Ibid.*, p. 279.
8. *Ibid.*, p. 279.
9. *Ibid.*, p. 279.
10. *Ibid.*, XL (January 4, 1921), 9.
11. Cf. *Ibid.*, XLII (June 19, 1923), 202.
12. *Ibid.*, p. 202.

13. *Ibid.,* XL (August 30, 1921), 279.
14. *Ibid.,* XL (January 4, 1921), 9.
15. *The Lutheran,* III (May 19, 1921), 17.
16. *Ibid.,* III (February 17, 1921), 17.
17. Cf. *Ibid.,* III (May 19, 1921), 17.
18. *Ibid.,* IX (March 3, 1927), 13.
19. *The Christian Advocate,* LXXXI (September 10, 1920), 1156.
20. *The Watchman-Examiner,* IX[2] (October 20, 1921), 1327.
21. *The Christian Advocate,* LXXXII (September 16, 1921), 1156.
22. *Ibid.,* p. 1156.
23. *Ibid.,* p. 1156.
24. *Ibid.,* p. 1156.
25. *The American Hebrew,* CVIII (December 10, 1920), 136.
26. *Ibid.,* p. 136.
27. *The Christian Advocate,* LXXXIV (June 1, 1923), 693.
28. *Ibid.,* p. 693.
29. *Ibid.,* LXXXI (May 21, 1920), 644.
30. *Ibid.,* LXXXV (March 28, 1924), 389.
31. *Ibid.,* LXXXIII (April 7, 1922), 420.
32. Cf. *Ibid.,* LXXXVII (March 12, 1926), 324.
33. *Ibid.,* LXXXII (January 21, 1921), 85.
34. *Ibid.,* p. 85.
35. *Ibid.,* LXXXII (September 2, 1921), 1109.
36. *Ibid.,* LXXXIII (January 20, 1922), 85.
37. *Ibid.,* LXXXIV (February 23, 1923), 231.
38. *Ibid.,* p. 231.
39. *Ibid.,* LXXXIII (February 10, 1922), 164.
40. *The American Hebrew,* CVIII (March 25, 1921), 522.
41. *The Word and Way,* LXIV (March 1, 1928), 2.
42. *Ibid.,* p. 2.
43. *Ibid.,* p. 2.
44. *Ibid.,* p. 2.
45. *Ibid.,* p. 2.
46. Cf. *Ibid.,* p. 2.
47. *Ibid.,* LXIII (January 20, 1927), 2.
48. *Ibid.,* p. 2.
49. *Ibid.,* LXIV (March 29, 1928), 2.
50. *The Baptist,* IV (July 28, 1923), 804.
51. *Ibid.,* p. 804.
52. Cf. *Ibid.,* p. 804.
53. *The Watchman-Examiner,* VIII[1] (March 11, 1920), 337.
54. *Ibid.,* p. 337.
55. *Ibid.,* p. 337.
56. *Ibid.,* X[2] (September 28, 1922), 1231.
57. *Ibid.,* p. 1231.
58. *Ibid.,* p. 1231.
59. Cf. *The Christian Register,* C (April 7, 1921), 315.
60. *The Presbyterian Banner,* CXIII (September 16, 1926), 9.
61. *Ibid.,* p. 9.
62. *The Living Church,* LXVI (February 25, 1922), 538.
63. *Ibid.,* p. 538.

64. *The Christian Advocate*, LXXXII (October 14, 1921), 1284.
65. *Ibid.*, p. 1284.
66. *The Lutheran*, V (September 20, 1923), 15.

CHAPTER VII

1. Cf. P. W. Slosson, *op. cit.*, p. 151.
2. *The Lutheran*, II (July 22, 1920), 196.
3. Cf. *Ibid.*, p. 196.
4. *Ibid.*, p. 196.
5. *Lutheran Witness*, XLI (February 28, 1922), 74.
6. *Ibid.*, XL (May 24, 1921), 168.
7. Cf. *Ibid.*, p. 168.
8. *Ibid.*, XLI (February 28, 1922), 74.
9. *The Living Church*, LXXX (November 3, 1928), 13.
10. *Ibid.*, p. 13.
11. *Ibid.*, p. 13.
12. *Ibid.*, p. 13.
13. Cf. *Ibid.*, p. 13.
14. *Ibid.*, LXXV (September 4, 1926), 631.
15. *Ibid.*, p. 631.
16. *Ibid.*, LXXX (January 26, 1929), 441.
17. Cf. *Ibid.*, LXIII (July 3, 1920), 331.
18. *Ibid.*, LXXV (September 4, 1926), 631.
19. *The Christian Advocate*, LXXXI (May 28, 1920), 675.
20. *Ibid.*, p. 675.
21. *Ibid.*, p. 675.
22. *Ibid.*, LXXXII (January 28, 1921), 99.
23. *Ibid.*, p. 99.
24. *Ibid.*, LXXXIII (July 14, 1922), 885.
25. Cf. *Ibid.*, LXXXII (April 1, 1921), 399.
26. *Ibid.*, p. 399.
27. Cf. *Ibid.*, LXXXII (January 14, 1921), 35.
28. *The Baptist*, IV (February 17, 1923), 71.
29. Cf. *The Living Church*, LXIII (July 3, 1920), 331.
30. Cf. *The Christian Advocate*, LXXXIII (July 14, 1922), 868.
31. *The Baptist*, VIII[1] (January 8, 1927), 39.
32. *The Christian Advocate*, LXXXIX (March 30, 1928), 389.
33. Cf. Percival White, "Figuring Us Out," *North American Review*, CCXXVII (1929), 69.
34. Cf. Rose Feld, "The Cosmetic Urge," *Collier's*, LXXIX (March 12, 1927), 22.
35. *The Presbyterian Banner*, CXIII (November 25, 1926), 9.
36. *Ibid.*, p. 9.
37. *The Lutheran*, II (July 22, 1920), 196.
38. *Ibid.*, p. 196.
39. *The Watchman-Examiner*, XV[2] (November 3, 1927), 1383.
40. Cf. *The Christian Register*, C (August 29, 1921), 713.
41. *Ibid.*, p. 713.
42. *Ibid.*, p. 713.
43. *Ibid.*, p. 713.
44. *The American Hebrew*, CXXIV (April 19, 1929), 825.
45. *Ibid.*, p. 825.

46. Cf. Dept. of Commerce, *Statistical Abstract of the United States for 1925*, pp. 757-759.
47. *The Christian Advocate*, LXXXII (February 4, 1921), 131.
48. *The Christian Advocate*, N. Y., CIV (December 26, 1929), 1584.
49. *Ibid.*, p. 1584.
50. *Ibid.*, CIV (March 21, 1929), 357.
51. *The Christian Advocate*, XC (April 26, 1929), 516.
52. *Ibid.*, LXXXII (June 24, 1921), 789.
53. *The American Hebrew*, CVI (January 23, 1920), 293.
54. *Ibid.*, p. 293.
55. *The Presbyterian Magazine*, XXVIII (May, 1922), 291.
56. *Ibid.*, p. 291.
57. Quoted in *The Christian Advocate*, LXXXIII (June 23, 1922), 771.
58. *The Lutheran*, XI (April 11, 1929), 3.
59. *Ibid.*, p. 3.
60. *Ibid.*, p. 3.
61. Cf. *Ibid.*, IV (June 8, 1922), 3.
62. Cf. *The Watchman-Examiner*, XIII[1] (February 12, 1925), 199; also Cf. *Ibid.*, XIII[1] (May 28, 1925), 679, and *Ibid.*, XIV[1] (April 22, 1926), 489.
63. *Ibid.*, XIV[1] (April 22, 1926), 489.
64. *The Baptist*, VIII[2] (July 9, 1927), 899.
65. Cf. *Ibid.*, X[1] (February 23, 1929), 257.
66. *Ibid.*, X[1] (April 6, 1929), 450.
67. *Ibid.*, X[1] (February 23, 1929), 257.
68. *The Commonweal*, V (November 24, 1926), 64.
69. *Ibid.*, p. 64.
70. *Ibid.*, p. 64.
71. *America*, XXXV (May 29, 1926), 161.
72. *Ibid.*, XL (November 3, 1928), 79.
73. *Ibid.*, p. 79.
74. Cf. *Ibid.*, p. 79.
75. *Ibid.*, XLI (July 27, 1929), 365.
76. *Ibid.*, XL (November 3, 1928), 79.
77. Cf. *The Christian Register*, CI (May 25, 1922), 493.
78. *Ibid.*, CVIII (August 22, 1929), 697.
79. *Ibid.*, p. 697.
80. *Ibid.*, CVIII (June 20, 1929), 529.
81. *Ibid.*, CVIII (August 22, 1929), 697.
82. *Ibid.*, CIII (July 24, 1924), 703.

CHAPTER VIII

1. *Lutheran Witness*, XLIV (March 24, 1925), 98.
2. *Ibid.*, p. 98.
3. *Ibid.*, p. 98.
4. Cf. *The Lutheran*, I (April 15, 1920), 990.
5. *Ibid.*, p. 990.
6. *Ibid.*, IV (December 8, 1921), 16.
7. *Ibid.*, VI (August 14, 1924), 14.
8. Cf. *Ibid.*, p. 14.
9. *The Christian Advocate*, LXXXV (February 8, 1924), 166.
10. *Ibid.*, LXXXV (February 29, 1924), 259.
11. Cf. *Ibid.*, p. 259.

12. *Ibid.,* LXXXV (July 4, 1924), 835.
13. *Ibid.,* LXXXII (March 25, 1921), 372.
14. *Ibid.,* LXXXII (March 4, 1921), 277.
15. *Ibid.,* LXXXIV (January 12, 1923), 37.
16. *Ibid.,* p. 37.
17. *The Christian Advocate,* N. Y., XCVI (April 28, 1921), 540.
18. *Ibid.,* p. 540.
19. *Ibid.,* p. 540.
20. *Ibid.,* XCVI (May 12, 1921), 612.
21. *Ibid.,* p. 612.
22. *Ibid.,* XCV² (November 18, 1920), 1152.
23. Cf. *Ibid.,* p. 1152.
24. Cf. *The Baptist,* II (February 5, 1921), 6.
25. *Ibid.,* p. 6.
26. Cf. *Ibid.,* II (October 8, 1921), 1135.
27. *Ibid.,* I² (January 22, 1921), 1734.
28. *Ibid.,* p. 1734.
29. Cf. *Ibid.,* X² (November 16, 1929), 1400.
30. Cf. *Ibid.,* 1¹ (February 14, 1920), 81.
31. Cf. *The Word and Way,* LXIV (October 20, 1927), 2.
32. *Ibid.,* p. 2.
33. *The Watchman-Examiner,* XIV² (July 15, 1926), 866.
34. *Ibid.,* XIII¹ (May 14, 1925), 613.
35. *Ibid.,* p. 613.
36. *Ibid.,* p. 613.
37. *Ibid.,* IX¹ (March 31, 1921), 390.
38. *Ibid.,* p. 390.
39. Cf. *Ibid.,* p. 390.
40. *Ibid.,* p. 390.
41. *The Presbyterian Banner,* CVII (March 10, 1921), 1028.
42. *New Era Magazine,* XXVII¹ (May, 1921), 322.
43. Cf. *The Presbyterian Magazine,* XXX (August, 1924), 381.
44. *The Living Church,* LXVI (February 25, 1922), 543.
45. *Ibid.,* p. 543.
46. Cf. *Ibid.,* p. 543.
47. *Ibid.,* p. 543.
48. *The American-Hebrew,* CXVI (February 27, 1925), 465.
49. *Ibid.,* p. 465.
50. *Ibid.,* CVIII (April 8, 1921), 566.
51. Cf. *Ibid.,* p. 566.
52. *Ibid.,* p. 566.
53. *The Christian Register,* XCIX (January 22, 1920), 86.
54. *Ibid.,* p. 86.
55. Cf. *Ibid.,* p. 86.
56. *Ibid.,* CVIII (August 1, 1929), 648.
57. *Ibid.,* C (July 28, 1921), 699.
58. Cf. *Ibid.,* p. 699.
59. Cf. *America,* XXXI (June 28, 1924), 249.
60. *Ibid.,* p. 249.
61. *Ibid.,* XXXI (August 2, 1924), 379.
62. *Ibid.,* XXXI (August 30, 1924), 474.
63. *The Commonweal,* IV (May 12, 1926), 7, 8.

CHAPTER IX

1. *The Presbyterian Magazine*, XXXI (May, 1925), 228.
2. Cf. *Ibid.*, p. 228.
3. Cf. *Ibid.*, XXVIII (May, 1922), 291.
4. *The Presbyterian Banner*, CVIII (January 18, 1922), 2371.
5. Cf. *The Lutheran*, VII (October 23, 1924), 14, 15.
6. *Ibid.*, p. 15.
7. *Ibid.*, p. 15.
8. Cf. *The Watchman-Examiner*, XII² (October 2, 1924), 1271.
9. *Ibid.*, p. 1271.
10. *The Baptist*, I² (January 1, 1921), 1639.
11. Cf. *America*, XXXIV (January 9, 1926), 297.
12. *Ibid.*, p. 297.
13. Cf. *The Commonweal*, IV (September 29, 1926), 487.
14. *Ibid.*, III (April 14, 1926), 620.
15. *America*, XXXI (September 20, 1924), 546.
16. *Ibid.*, XXXVII (September 10, 1927), 511.
17. *Ibid.*, p. 511.
18. *Ibid.*, p. 511.
19. *The Christian Register*, CIV (August 27, 1925), 835.
20. Cf. *Ibid.*, CVIII (January 17, 1929), 49.
21. *Ibid.*, p. 49.
22. *Ibid.*, CIV (August 27, 1925), 835.
23. Cf. *The Christian Advocate*, XC (September 27, 1929), 1219.
24. *Ibid.*, p. 1219.
25. *Ibid.*, LXXXVI (August 14, 1925), 1123.
26. *Ibid.*, p. 1123.
27. *The Christian Advocate*, N. Y., C (July 9, 1925), 868.
28. Cf. *Ibid.*, p. 868.
29. Cf. *The Living Church*, LXXIII (July 4, 1925), 327.
30. Cf. *Lutheran Witness*, XLIV (October 6, 1925), 322, 323.
31. *The Commonweal*, III (April 28, 1926), 676.
32. *Ibid.*, p. 676.
33. Cf. *The Watchman-Examiner*, XIV² (October 28, 1926), 1351.
34. *The Baptist*, V (October 11, 1924), 878.
35. *The Christian Advocate*, LXXXIV (November 2, 1923), 1379.
36. Cf. *Ibid.*, p. 1379.
37. *Ibid.*, LXXXIV (March 23, 1923), 356.
38. *The Christian Advocate*, N. Y., XCVI (February 17, 1921), 203.
39. Cf. *The Christian Advocate*, LXXXIII (March 10, 1922), 309.
40. *The Christian Advocate*, N. Y., XCVI (February 17, 1921), 203.
41. *America*, XXXVI (February 19, 1927), 444, 445.
42. *Ibid.*, p. 444.
43. *Ibid.*, p. 445.
44. Cf. *The Lutheran*, IX (April 21, 1927), 15.
45. *Ibid.*, p. 15.
46. *The Christian Advocate*, LXXXIII (March 24, 1922), 357.
47. *Ibid.*, LXXXVIII (March 25, 1927), 355.
48. *Ibid.*, p. 355.
49. Cf. *Ibid.*, p. 355.
50. *The Baptist*, I² (July 31, 1920), 937.
51. Cf. *Ibid.*, p. 937.

52. *Ibid.*, p. 937.
53. Cf. *Ibid.*, p. 937.
54. *The Presbyterian Banner*, CXIII (March 17, 1927), 9.
55. Cf. *Ibid.*, p. 9.
56. *Ibid.*, p. 9.
57. Cf. *Ibid.*, p. 9.
58. *The Christian Register*, CIII (May 4, 1924), 459.
59. *Ibid.*, p. 459.
60. *Ibid.*, p. 459.
61. Cf. P. W. Slosson, *op. cit.*, p. 95.

CHAPTER X

1. *Literary Digest*, CIII (November 23, 1929), p. 24.
2. *The Journal of Social Hygiene*, (April, 1927), p. 227.
3. J. M. Gilette, "Family Life," *American Year Book for 1925*, p. 665. "Term marriage" existed whenever a divorce was taken for granted if the venture did not turn out happily. If it were entered upon with no expectation of children, the term marriage became companionate marriage. Cf., B. B. Lindsey and Wainright Evans, *The Companionate Marriage*, N. Y., 1927.
4. *The Christian Register*, CVI (December 1, 1927), 946.
5. *Ibid.*, p. 946.
6. *Ibid.*, p. 946.
7. Cf. *Ibid.*, p. 946.
8. *Ibid.*, p. 946.
9. Cf. *Ibid.*, CVI (August 25, 1927), 670.
10. *Ibid.*, p. 670.
11. *Ibid.*, p. 670.
12. *Ibid.*, p. 670.
13. *The Living Church*, LXXVIII (December 10, 1927), 185.
14. *Ibid.*, p. 185.
15. Cf. *Ibid.*, LXXVI (February 19, 1927), 555.
16. *The Christian Register*, CVI (June 7, 1927), 551.
17. *Ibid.*, p. 551.
18. *Ibid.*, p. 551.
19. *Ibid.*, p. 551.
20. *The Presbyterian Banner*, CXIV (December 1, 1927), 8.
21. Cf. *Ibid.*, p. 8.
22. *Ibid.*, CXIV (March 1, 1928), 8.
23. *Ibid.*, p. 8.
24. Cf. *Ibid.*, p. 8.
25. *America*, XXXVIII (February 4, 1928), 407.
26. Cf. *Ibid.*, XXXVIII (December 17, 1927), 230.
27. *The Commonweal*, V (April 6, 1927), 594.
28. *Ibid.*, p. 594.
29. *Ibid.*, VII (November 23, 1927), 711.
30. *Ibid.*, p. 711.
31. *Ibid.*, p. 711.
32. *Ibid.*, p. 711.
33. *Ibid.*, VII (December 7, 1927), 775.
34. *America*, XXXIX (September 1, 1928), 486.
35. Cf. *The Christian Advocate*, N. Y., CIII (February 23, 1928), 228, 229.

36. *Ibid.,* p. 229.
37. *Ibid.,* CII (July 28, 1927), 916, 917.
38. *Ibid.,* p. 917.
39. Cf. *Lutheran Witness,* XLVII (May 15, 1928), 175.
40. *Ibid.,* XLVI (December 13, 1927), 433.
41. *The Lutheran,* IV (March 23, 1922), 17.
42. *Ibid.,* IX (March 17, 1927), 14.
43. Cf. *Ibid.,* p. 14.
44. *Ibid.,* p. 14.
45. Cf. *Ibid.,* p. 14.
46. Cf. *The Baptist,* VIII[1] (March 19, 1927), 375.
47. Cf. *The Word and Way,* LXIII (June 9, 1927), 5.
48. *Ibid.,* p. 5.
49. *The Watchman-Examiner,* XVI[2] (September 20, 1928), 1193.
50. Cf. *The American Hebrew,* CXX (February 4, 1927), 429.

CHAPTER XI

1. *Genesis,* 38, 9.
2. Cf. L. M. Miller, "Margaret Sanger: Mother of Planned Parenthood," *Reader's Digest* (July, 1951), 27-31.
3. *Lutheran Witness,* XLII (May 22, 1923), 161.
4. Cf. *Ibid.,* p. 161.
5. *The Lutheran,* X (October 6, 1927), 15.
6. *Ibid.,* p. 15.
7. *Lutheran Witness,* XLIII (May 20, 1924), 199.
8. *Ibid.,* p. 199.
9. *Ibid.,* p. 199.
10. *Ibid.,* p. 199.
11. *Ibid.,* p. 199.
12. *America,* XXXII (December 6, 1924), 184.
13. *Ibid.,* p. 184.
14. *Ibid.,* XXXVIII (February 18, 1928), 455.
15. *Ibid.,* XXXII (December 6, 1924), 184.
16. Cf. *Ibid.,* XL (March 9, 1929), 517.
17. *Ibid.,* p. 517.
18. *Ibid.,* XLII (November 23, 1929), 151.
19. *Ibid.,* XXXVIII (February 18, 1928), 455.
20. *The Commonweal,* I (February 18, 1925), 396.
21. *Ibid.,* p. 396.
22. *Ibid.,* p. 396.
23. *America,* XXXII (April 4, 1925), 591, 592.
24. *The Commonweal,* I (February 18, 1925), 396.
25. Cf. *Ibid.,* III (April 7, 1926), 594.
26. *Ibid.,* III (February 24, 1926), 427.
27. *Ibid.,* I (April 15, 1925), 618.
28. *The Living Church,* LXXVII (July 16, 1927), 357.
29. *The Christian Register,* CVIII (July 4, 1929), 567, 568.
30. *Ibid.,* p. 568.
31. *Ibid.,* CVIII (May 30, 1929), 471.
32. *The Watchman-Examiner,* XIV[2] (December 16, 1926), 1577.
33. *Ibid.,* XVII[1] (March 15, 1928), 322.
34. *Ibid.,* p. 322.

35. *The Christian Advocate*, N. Y., XCVI (December 1, 1921), 1515.
36. *Ibid.*, p. 1515.
37. *Ibid.*, p. 1515.
38. Oscar T. Barck and Nelson M. Blake, *Since 1900*. (New York: Macmillan and Co., 1949), p. 181.
39. *Casti Connubii*. Discussion Club Outline. (New York: Paulist Press, 1941), p. 17.
40. Cf. Dr. Marynia F. Farnham, "The Tragic Failure of America's Women," *Coronet*, XXII (September, 1947), 3-9.

CHAPTER XII

1. Charles H. Doyle, *Cana is Forever*. (New York: Nugent Press, 1949), p. 204.
2. Cf. P. W. Slosson, *op. cit.*, p. 142.
3. Cf. Frederick Lewis Allen, *Only Yesterday*. (New York: Harper and Brothers, 1931), p. 116.
4. *America*, XLI (June 22, 1929), 245, 246.
5. *Lutheran*, IV (September 21, 1922), 16.
6. Cf. *Christian Register*, CI (March 16, 1922), 243.
7. *The Christian Advocate*, LXXXII (June 24, 1921), 772.
8. *The Watchman-Examiner*, XVII² (July 4, 1929), 841.
9. *The Christian Advocate*, LXXXI (April 16, 1920), 485.
10. Cf. *Ibid.*, p. 485.
11. Cf. *Ibid.*, LXXXI (May 7, 1920), 580.
12. Cf. *Ibid.*, p. 580.
13. *Ibid.*, LXXXII (June 24, 1921), 772.
14. Cf. *Ibid.*, LXXXV (January 18, 1924), 71.
15. *Ibid.*, XC (April 12, 1929), 452.
16. *Ibid.*, XC (June 7, 1929), 707.
17. *The Christian Advocate*, N. Y., XCV² (August 19, 1920), 1107.
18. *Ibid.*, p. 1107.
19. *Ibid.*, p. 1107.
20. *Ibid.*, p. 1107.
21. P. W. Slosson, *op. cit.*, p. 143.
22. *The Presbyterian Banner*, CXIII (February 10, 1927), 5.
23. *The American Hebrew*, CVIII (April 8, 1921), 565.
24. Cf. *Ibid.*, p. 565.
25. *Ibid.*, CVI (May 14, 1920), 849.
26. Cf. *The Living Church*, LXIV (January 22, 1921), 387, 388.
27. *Ibid.*, LXIV (February 26, 1921), 526.
28. *Ibid.*, LXIX (June 23, 1923), 248.
29. *Ibid.*, p. 248.
30. *The Christian Register*, XCIX (July 22, 1920), 710.
31. *Ibid.*, p. 710.
32. *Ibid.*, p. 710.
33. *Ibid.*, p. 710.
34. *The Christian Register*, CVI (December 8, 1927), 967.
35. Cf. *Ibid.*, p. 967.
36. *Ibid.*, p. 967.
37. Cf. *Ibid.*, XCIX (July 22, 1920), 710.
38. *Ibid.*, p. 710.
39. *Lutheran Witness*, XL (September 13, 1921), 293.

40. Cf. *Ibid.,* p. 293.
41. *Ibid.,* XLVI (November 29, 1927), 410.
42. *Ibid.,* p. 410.
43. Cf. *Ibid.,* p. 410.
44. *Ibid.,* p. 410.
45. *Ibid.,* p. 410.
46. *The Lutheran,* IV (February 9, 1922), 16, 17.
47. Cf. *Ibid.,* p. 17.
48. *Ibid.,* III (October 7, 1920), 17.
49. Cf. *Ibid.,* p. 17.
50. *Ibid.,* p. 17.
51. *Ibid.,* VII (April 23, 1925), 15.
52. *The Watchman-Examiner,* VIII^2 (September 23, 1920), 1158.
53. *Ibid.,* IX^2 (October 13, 1921), 1291.
54. *The Baptist,* II (February 12, 1921), 38.
55. Cf. *Ibid.,* p. 38.
56. *Ibid.,* p. 38.
57. Cf. *The Commonweal,* I (March 11, 1925), 480.
58. *Ibid.,* p. 480.
59. *America,* XXXVII (May 28, 1927), 150, 151.
60. Cf. *Ibid.,* p. 150.
61. *Ibid.,* XXXI (July 26, 1924), 354.
62. Cf. *Ibid.,* XXXIII (May 16, 1925), 113.
63. *Ibid.,* XXXVI (December 11, 1926), 201.
64. Cf. *Ibid.,* XXXVIII (December 3, 1927), 175.
65. Cf. *Ibid.,* p. 175.
66. *Ibid.,* p. 175.
67. Cf. *Ibid.,* XXXIX (October 6, 1928), 606, 607.
68. *Ibid.,* XXXVI (December 11, 1926), 201.

APPENDIX A

1. Hansen, Harry (ed.). *The World Almanac and Book of Facts.* (New York: 1928), p. 305.
2. Hansen, Harry (ed.). *The World Almanac and Book of Facts.* (New York: 1937), p. 432.
3. 1926—All Jews in communities where there is a congregation. 1916 (heads of families, seat holders and other contributors, but admittedly incomplete.)
4. Hansen, Harry (ed.). *The World Almanac and Book of Facts.* (New York: 1953), p. 437.
5. Hansen, Harry (ed.). *The World Almanac and Book of Facts.* (New York: 1932), p. 443.
6. Hansen, Harry (ed.). *The World Almanac and Book of Facts.* (New York: 1953), p. 437.

Bibliography

BIBLIOGRAPHICAL GUIDES

Child, H. L. *A Reference Guide to the Study of Public Opinion.* Princeton: Princeton University Press, 1934.

Meier, J. H. (ed.). *Catholic Press Directory for 1923.* Chicago.

Smith, Bruce L. *Propaganda, Communication, and Public Opinion.* Princeton: Princeton University Press, 1946.

PRIMARY SOURCES

Periodicals

This study has depended on periodicals as the principal source. The following magazines are recognized as officially representative of the respective religious denominations. Every periodical, with the exception of the *Presbyterian Magazine* and the *Lutheran Witness,* is a weekly publication. It will be seen thus that more than 6500 issues of the following journals were examined. Listed below are specific citations on issues which supplied material directly for incorporation into this study.

America. XXXI (June 28, 1924), 249.
———. XXXI (July 26, 1924), 354.
———. XXXI (August 2, 1924), 379.
———. XXXI (August 30, 1924), 474.
———. XXXI (September 13, 1924), 513.
———. XXXI (September 20, 1924), 546.
———. XXXI (September 27, 1924), 571.
———. XXXII (October 18, 1924), 15.
———. XXXII (December 6, 1924), 184.
———. XXXII (April 4, 1925), 591, 592.
———. XXXIII (May 16, 1925), 113.
———. XXXIV (January 9, 1926), 297.
———. XXXIV (January 16, 1926), 320.
———. XXXIV (January 23, 1926), 343.

————. XXXV (May 29, 1926), 161.
————. XXXV (July 10, 1926), 294.
————. XXXV (October 2, 1926), 591.
————. XXXVI (November 13, 1926), 103.
————. XXXVI (December 11, 1926), 201.
————. XXXVI (February 19, 1927), 444, 445.
————. XXXVII (May 28, 1927), 150, 151.
————. XXXVII (August 20, 1927), 447.
————. XXXVII (September 10, 1927), 511.
————. XXXVIII (December 3, 1927), 175.
————. XXXVIII (December 17, 1927), 230.
————. XXXVIII (December 31, 1927), 286.
————. XXXVIII (February 4, 1928), 407.
————. XXXVIII (February 18, 1928), 455.
————. XXXIX (September 1, 1928), 486.
————. XXXIX (October 6, 1928), 606, 607.
————. XL (November 3, 1928), 79.
————. XL (March 9, 1929), 517.
————. XLI (June 22, 1929), 245, 246.
————. XLI (July 27, 1929), 365.
————. XLII (November 23, 1929), 151.
American Hebrew, The. CVI (January 23, 1920), 293.
————. CVI (April 9, 1920), 694.
————. CVI (May 14, 1920), 849.
————. CVIII (December 10, 1920), 136.
————. CVIII (March 25, 1921), 522.
————. CVIII (April 8, 1921), 565, 566.
————. CXI (November 10, 1922), 685.
————. CXIV (January 4, 1924), 233.
————. CXVI (February 27, 1925), 465.
————. CXVIII (January 15, 1926), 321.
————. CXX (February 4, 1927), 429.
————. CXXIV (April 19, 1929), 825.
Baptist, The. I^1 (January 31, 1920), 8.
————. I^1 (February 14, 1920), 81.
————. I^1 (February 21, 1920), 116.
————. I^2 (July 31, 1920), 937.
————. I^2 (August 7, 1920), 965.
————. I^2 (October 23, 1920), 1320.
————. I^2 (December 11, 1920), 1577.
————. I^2 (January 1, 1921), 1639.
————. I^2 (January 22, 1921), 1734.
————. II (February 5, 1921), 6.

————. II (February 12, 1921), 38.
————. II (March 26, 1921), 229.
————. II (July 16, 1921), 750.
————. II (October 8, 1921), 1135.
————. III (February 24, 1922), 73.
————. III (March 4, 1922), 134.
————. III (July 1, 1922), 681, 682.
————. III (August 19, 1922), 883.
————. III (November 11, 1922), 1266.
————. IV (February 17, 1923), 71.
————. IV (May 12, 1923), 455.
————. IV (July 28, 1923), 804.
————. V (October 11, 1924), 878.
————. V (October 18, 1924), 902.
————. VIII^1 (January 8, 1927), 39.
————. VIII^1 (March 19, 1927), 375.
————. VIII^1 (April 16, 1927), 503.
————. VIII^2 (July 9, 1927), 899.
————. VIII^2 (July 23, 1927), 955.
————. IX^1 (April 28, 1928), 527.
————. X^1 (February 23, 1929), 257.
————. X^1 (March 9, 1929), 312.
————. X^1 (April 6, 1929), 450.
————. X^2 (October 12, 1929), 1290.
————. X^2 (November 16, 1929), 1400.
Christian Advocate, The. LXXXI (April 16, 1920), 485.
————. LXXXI (May 7, 1920), 580.
————. LXXXI (May 21, 1920), 644.
————. LXXXI (May 28, 1920), 675.
————. LXXXI (August 27, 1920), 1093.
————. LXXXI (September 10, 1920), 1156.
————. LXXXI (November 5, 1920), 1411, 1429.
————. LXXXI (December 17, 1920), 1603.
————. LXXXII (January 14, 1921), 35.
————. LXXXII (January 21, 1921), 85.
————. LXXXII (January 28, 1921), 99.
————. LXXXII (February 4, 1921), 131.
————. LXXXII (February 18, 1921), 195.
————. LXXXII (March 4, 1921), 277.
————. LXXXII (March 25, 1921), 372.
————. LXXXII (April 1, 1921), 399.
————. LXXXII (June 24, 1921), 772, 789.
————. LXXXII (September 2, 1921), 1109.

———. LXXXII (September 16, 1921), 1156.
———. LXXXII (October 14, 1921), 1284.
———. LXXXIII (January 20, 1922), 85.
———. LXXXIII (February 10, 1922), 164.
———. LXXXIII (March 10, 1922), 309.
———. LXXXIII (March 24, 1922), 357.
———. LXXXIII (April 7, 1922), 420.
———. LXXXIII (June 9, 1922), 707.
———. LXXXIII (June 23, 1922), 771.
———. LXXXIII (July 14, 1922), 868, 885.
———. LXXXIII (July 28, 1922), 931.
———. LXXXIII (September 22, 1922), 1187.
———. LXXXIII (December 1, 1922), 1508.
———. LXXXIV (January 12, 1923), 37.
———. LXXXIV (February 23, 1923), 231.
———. LXXXIV (March 23, 1923), 356.
———. LXXXIV (May 4, 1923), 565.
———. LXXXIV (June 1, 1923), 693.
———. LXXXIV (June 15, 1923), 755.
———. LXXXIV (June 22, 1923), 788.
———. LXXXIV (August 3, 1923), 981.
———. LXXXIV (November 2, 1923), 1379.
———. LXXXV (January 18, 1924), 71.
———. LXXXV (February 8, 1924), 166.
———. LXXXV (February 29, 1924), 259.
———. LXXXV (March 28, 1924), 389.
———. LXXXV (July 4, 1924), 835.
———. LXXXV (October 10, 1924), 1283.
———. LXXXVI (May 1, 1925), 645.
———. LXXXVI (August 14, 1925), 1123.
———. LXXXVII (March 12, 1926), 324.
———. LXXXVIII (March 25, 1927), 355.
———. LXXXVIII (June 10, 1927), 708.
———. LXXXVIII (December 16, 1927), 1572.
———. LXXIX (March 30, 1928), 389.
———. XC (April 12, 1929), 452.
———. XC (April 26, 1929), 516.
———. XC (June 7, 1929), 707.
———. XC (September 27, 1929), 1219.
Christian Advocate, The, (New York), XCV² (July 15, 1920), 948.
———. XCV² (August 19, 1920), 1107.
———. XCV² (October 28, 1920), 1426.
———. XCV² (November 18, 1920), 1152.

————. XCVI (January 13, 1921), 34.
————. XCVI (January 20, 1921), 67.
————. XCVI (January 27, 1921), 99, 100.
————. XCVI (February 17, 1921), 203.
————. XCVI (April 28, 1921), 540.
————. XCVI (May 12, 1921), 612.
————. XCVI (December 1, 1921), 1515.
————. XCVIII (May 24, 1923), 646.
————. C (January 15, 1925), 71.
————. C (April 30, 1925), 549.
————. C (June 25, 1925), 805.
————. C (July 9, 1925), 868.
————. C (September 10, 1925), 1091.
————. C (October 15, 1925), 1254.
————. C (November 26, 1925), 1445.
————. CI (January 14, 1926), 38.
————. CI (April 15, 1926), 454.
————. CI (August 26, 1926), 1020.
————. CII (April 21, 1927), 485.
————. CII (July 28, 1927), 916, 917.
————. CIII (February 23, 1928), 228, 229.
————. CIII (December 6, 1928), 1493.
————. CIV (January 17, 1929), 69.
————. CIV (March 21, 1929), 357.
————. CIV (December 26, 1929), 1584.
Christian Register, The. XCIX (January 22, 1920), 86.
————. XCIX (July 22, 1920), 710.
————. XCIX (October 7, 1920), 975.
————. C (February 24, 1921), 171.
————. C (April 7, 1921), 315.
————. C (May 19, 1921), 459.
————. C (July 28, 1921), 699.
————. C (August 29, 1921), 713.
————. C (October 13, 1921), 963.
————. CI (March 16, 1922), 243.
————. CI (April 20, 1922), 367.
————. CI (May 25, 1922), 493.
————. CII (April 26, 1923), 387.
————. CIII (January 31, 1924), 107.
————. CIII (May 4, 1924), 459.
————. CIII (July 24, 1924), 703.
————. CIII (August 28, 1924), 823.
————. CIII (November 27, 1924), 1139.

———. CIV (February 26, 1925), 195.
———. CIV (April 9, 1925), 339.
———. CIV (August 27, 1925), 835.
———. CIV (October 22, 1925), 1026.
———. CV (February 16, 1926), 1131.
———. CV (May 27, 1926), 487.
———. CV (September 23, 1926), 858.
———. CV (October 7, 1926), 903.
———. CVI (February 10, 1927), 106.
———. CVI (June 7, 1927), 551.
———. CVI (June 30, 1927), 580.
———. CVI (August 25, 1927), 670.
———. CVI (December 1, 1927), 946.
———. CVI (December 8, 1927), 967.
———. CVII (January 19, 1928), 42, 43.
———. CVII (August 31, 1928), 691.
———. CVIII (January 17, 1929), 49.
———. CVIII (May 30, 1929), 471.
———. CVIII (June 20, 1929), 529.
———. CVIII (July 4, 1929), 567, 568.
———. CVIII (August 1, 1929), 648.
———. CVIII (August 22, 1929), 697.
Commonweal, The. I (February 18, 1925), 395, 396.
———. I (March 11, 1925), 480.
———. I (April 15, 1925), 618.
———. I (April 29, 1925), 670.
———. I (May 6, 1925), 697.
———. II (July 1, 1925), 202.
———. II (August 12, 1925), 320.
———. II (October 21, 1925), 579.
———. III (February 24, 1926), 426, 427.
———. III (April 7, 1926), 594.
———. III (April 14, 1926), 620, 621.
———. III (April 28, 1926), 676.
———. IV (May 12, 1926), 7, 8.
———. IV (September 29, 1926), 487.
———. IV (October 6, 1926), 516.
———. V (November 10, 1926), 2.
———. V (November 17, 1926), 36.
———. V (November 24, 1926), 64.
———. V (February 16, 1927), 398.
———. V (April 6, 1927), 594.
———. VII (November 23, 1927), 711.

———. VII (November 30, 1927), 746.

———. VII (December 7, 1927), 775.

———. VII (January 25, 1928), 970.

———. VII (February 1, 1928), 1000.

———. VIII (August 29, 1928), 401.

———. IX (November 14, 1928), 34.

———. X (August 21, 1929), 395.

———. X (September 25, 1929), 519.

———. XI (December 11, 1929), 157.

Living Church, The. LXIII (July 3, 1920), 331.

———. LXIII (July 24, 1920), 427.

———. LXIII (August 21, 1920), 555.

———. LXIV (November 6, 1920), 5.

———. LXIV (January 1, 1921), 280.

———. LXIV (January 22, 1921), 387, 388.

———. LXIV (February 26, 1921), 524, 526.

———. LXV (June 11, 1921), 170.

———. LXVI (February 25, 1922), 538, 543.

———. LXIX (May 19, 1923), 76.

———. LXIX (June 23, 1923), 248.

———. LXXI (October 4, 1924), 719.

———. LXXIII (July 4, 1925), 327.

———. LXXIII (July 18, 1925), 385.

———. LXXIV (April 24, 1926), 855.

———. LXXV (September 4, 1926), 631.

———. LXXVI (February 19, 1927), 555.

———. LXXVII (July 16, 1927), 357.

———. LXXVII (August 20, 1927), 531.

———. LXXVIII (December 10, 1927), 185.

———. LXXVIII (March 17, 1928), 661.

———. LXXIX (May 19, 1928), 77.

———. LXXX (November 3, 1928), 13.

———. LXXX (January 26, 1929), 441.

Lutheran, The. I (February 26, 1920), 872.

———. I (April 15, 1920), 990.

———. II (May 20, 1920), 34, 40.

———. II (July 22, 1920), 196.

———. II (August 12, 1920), 242.

———. III (October 7, 1920), 17.

———. III (December 23, 1920), 4.

———. III (February 17, 1921), 17.

——— III (May 19, 1921), 17.

———. III (July 28, 1921), 17.

————. IV (December 8, 1921), 16.
————. IV (January 5, 1922), 16.
————. IV (January 26, 1922), 16, 17.
————. IV (February 9, 1922), 16, 17.
————. IV (March 23, 1922), 17.
————. IV (June 8, 1922), 3.
————. IV (August 31, 1922), 3.
————. IV (September 21, 1922), 16.
————. V (September 20, 1923), 15.
————. VI (October 11, 1923), 17.
————. VI (March 27, 1924), 15.
————. VI (July 24, 1924), 15.
————. VI (August 14, 1924), 14.
————. VII (October 23, 1924), 14, 15.
————. VII (January 1, 1925), 15.
————. VII (April 23, 1925), 15.
————. VIII (October 15, 1925), 15.
————. VIII (May 6, 1926), 14.
————. VIII (September 16, 1926), 13.
————. IX (March 3, 1927), 13.
————. IX (March 17, 1927), 14.
————. IX (April 21, 1927), 15
————. IX (July 7, 1927), 3.
————. IX (September 15, 1927), 15.
————. IX (September 22, 1927), 14.
————. X (October 6, 1927), 15.
————. X (February 2, 1928), 4.
————. X (March 15, 1928), 3.
————. X (June 14, 1928), 3.
————. X (June 21, 1928), 3.
————. X (June 28, 1928), 3.
————. X (July 26, 1928), 4.
————. X (September 6, 1928), 12.
————. XI (December 27, 1928), 3.
————. XI (April 11, 1929), 3.
————. XI (September 5, 1929), 15.
————. XII (October 10, 1929), 4.
————. XII (November 7, 1929), 3.
Lutheran Witness. XXXIX (January 6, 1920), 5, 8.
————. XXXIX (January 20, 1920), 24.
————. XXXIX (February 3, 1920), 33.
————. XXXIX (March 16, 1920), 88.
————. XXXIX (August 17, 1920), 263.

————. XXXIX (August 31, 1920), 279.
————. XXXIX (November 23, 1920), 374, 375.
————. XXXIX (December 7, 1920), 391.
————. XL (January 4, 1921), 9.
————. XL (March 15, 1921), 88.
————. XL (March 29, 1921), 105.
————. XL (May 10, 1921), 152.
————. XL (May 24, 1921), 168.
————. XL (June 7, 1921), 185.
————. XL (August 30, 1921), 279.
————. XL (September 13, 1921), 293.
————. XLI (February 28, 1922), 74.
————. XLI (May 9, 1922), 145.
————. XLI (August 1, 1922), 245.
————. XLII (February 13, 1923), 53.
————. XLII (May 22, 1923), 161, 170, 199.
————. XLII (June 5, 1923), 178.
————. XLII (June 19, 1923), 202.
————. XLIII (January 15, 1924), 20.
————. XLIII (May 20, 1924), 199.
————. XLIII (August 12, 1924), 301.
————. XLIII (August 26, 1924), 316.
————. XLIV (January 27, 1925), 24.
————. XLIV (February 10, 1925), 38.
————. XLIV (March 10, 1925), 73.
————. XLIV (March 24, 1925), 98.
————. XLIV (October 6, 1925), 322, 323.
————. XLIV (December 15, 1925), 417.
————. XLV (October 19, 1926), 346.
————. XLVI (November 29, 1927), 410.
————. XLVI (December 13, 1927), 433.
————. XLVI (December 27, 1927), 452.
————. XLVII (March 20, 1928), 111.
————. XLVII (May 15, 1928), 175.
New Era Magazine, The (became *Presbyterian Magazine* in 1921).
————. XXVI (June, 1920), 407.
————. XXVII[1] (May, 1921), 322.
Presbyterian Banner, The. CVII (March 10, 1921), 1028.
————. CVIII (June 16, 1921), 1.
————. CVIII (July 7, 1921), 91.
————. CVIII (September 1, 1921), 283.
————. CVIII (January 18, 1922), 2371.
————. CIX (August 24, 1922), 1743.

———. CXII (November 26, 1925), 3.

———. CXII (May 27, 1926), 6.

———. CXIII (September 2, 1926), 9.

———. CXIII (September 16, 1926), 9.

———. CXIII (November 25, 1926), 9.

———. CXIII (January 20, 1927), 9.

———. CXIII (February 10, 1927), 5.

———. CXIII (March 17, 1927), 9.

———. CXIV (September 26, 1927), 11.

———. CXIV (October 20, 1927), 9.

———. CXIV (December 1, 1927), 8.

———. CXIV (March 1, 1928), 8.

Presbyterian Magazine, The. XXVII (March, 1922), 510.

———. XXVIII (May, 1922), 291, 771.

———. XXIX (February, 1923), 69.

———. XXIX (August, 1923), 435.

———. XXX (January, 1924), 28.

———. XXX (August, 1924), 381.

———. XXXI (February, 1925), 61.

———. XXXI (May, 1925), 228.

Watchman-Examiner, The. VIII[1] (March 11, 1920), 337.

———. VIII[2] (July 29, 1920), 951.

———. VIII[2] (September 23, 1920), 1158.

———. IX[1] (March 31, 1921), 390.

———. IX[1] (May 5, 1921), 548.

———. IX[2] (July 14, 1921), 871.

———. IX[2] (August 4, 1921), 973.

———. IX[2] (October 13, 1921), 1291.

———. IX[2] (October 20, 1921), 1327.

———. X[1] (March 9, 1922), 295.

———. X[1] (April 27, 1922), 519.

———. X[1] (May 11, 1922), 583.

———. X[1] (June 22, 1922), 773.

———. X[2] (September 28, 1922), 1231.

———. XI[2] (August 9, 1923), 1007.

———. XII[1] (February 28, 1924), 261.

———. XII[1] (March 13, 1924), 327.

———. XII[1] (June 5, 1924), 707.

———. XII[2] (July 24, 1924), 949.

———. XII[2] (August 14, 1924), 1047.

———. XII[2] (October 2, 1924), 1271.

———. XIII[1] (January 15, 1925), 71.

———. XIII[1] (February 12, 1925), 199.

———. XIII¹ (May 14, 1925), 613.

———. XIII¹ (May 28, 1925), 679.

———. XIII¹ (June 18, 1925), 783.

———. XIII² (November 12, 1925), 1453.

———. XIV¹ (February 11, 1926), 168.

———. XIV¹ (April 15, 1926), 455.

———. XIV¹ (April 22, 1926), 489.

———. XIV¹ (May 27, 1926), 644.

———. XIV² (July 15, 1926), 866.

———. XIV² (September 23, 1926), 1191.

———. XIV² (October 28, 1926), 1351.

———. XIV² (December 16, 1926), 1577.

———. XV¹ (May 5, 1927), 551.

———. XV² (November 3, 1927), 1383.

———. XV² (December 1, 1927), 1511.

———. XVI¹ (March 15, 1928), 322.

———. XVI² (September 20, 1928), 1193.

———. XVII¹ (January 10, 1929), 41.

———. XVII¹ (March 14, 1929), 329.

———. XVII² (July 4, 1929), 841.

———. XVII² (July 18, 1929), 898.

———. XVII² (August 22, 1929), 1065.

Word and Way, The. LXIII (January 20, 1927), 2.

———. LXIII (February 10, 1927), 3.

———. LXIII (April 7, 1927), 1.

———. LXIII (May 12, 1927), 2.

———. LXIII (June 9, 1927), 5.

———. LXIV (August 18, 1927), 2.

———. LXIV (October 20, 1927), 2.

———. LXIV (February 2, 1928), 2.

———. LXIV (February 9, 1928), 2.

———. LXIV (March 1, 1928), 2.

———. LXIV (March 29, 1928), 2.

———. LXIV (May 31, 1928), 2, 3.

———. LXV (July 5, 1928), 2.

———. LXV (October 4, 1928), 2.

SECONDARY SOURCES

Since this is a study on public opinion as reflected in the religious periodical press, books of a secondary nature have been but incidental. The following might be considered as directive as regards background placement for press utterances.

Books

Adams, James Truslow. *Our Business Civilization.* New York: Albert and Charles Boni, 1929.

Albid, William. *Public Opinion.* New York: McGraw-Hill Co., 1939.

Allen, Frederick Lewis. *Only Yesterday.* New York: Harper and Brothers, 1931.

Angell. Norman. *The Public Mind.* London, 1926.

Bailey, Thomas A. *The Man in the Street.* New York: Macmillan Co., 1948.

Baker, Ray S. *American Chronicle.* New York: Charles Scribner's Sons, 1945.

Barck, Oscar Theodore Jr., and Blake, Nelson Manfred. *Since 1900.* New York: Macmillan Co., 1949.

Barnays, Edward L. *Crystallizing Public Opinion.* New York: Boni and Liverwright, 1923.

Baumgartner, Appollinaris W. *Catholic Journalism.* New York: Columbia University Press, 1931.

Beard, Charles and Mary. *The American Period.* New York: Macmillan Co., 1942.

———. *The American Spirit.* New York: Macmillan Co., 1942.

———. *America in Mid-Passage.* New York: Macmillan Co., 1939.

Bleyer, W. G. *Main Currents in the History of American Journalism.* New York: Houghton Mifflin, 1927.

Bogardus, E. S. *The Making of Public Opinion.* New York: Association Press, 1950.

Brigham, Clarence Saunders. *Journals and Journeymen.* Philadelphia: University of Pennsylvania Press, 1950.

Cargill, Oscar. *Intellectual America: The March of Ideas.* New York: New York: Macmillan Co., 1941.

Clinthy, E. R. *All in the Name of God.* New York: John Day Co., 1934.

Cobb, Sanford H. *The Rise of Religious Liberty in America.* New York: Macmillan Co., 1902.

Cohn, David L. *Combustion on Wheels: An Informal History of the Automobile Age.* Boston: Houghton Mifflin Co., 1944.

———. *The Good Old Days.* New York: Simon Schuster, 1940.

Cox, George C. *The Public Conscience.* New York: Holt and Co., 1923.

Curti, Merle. *The Growth of American Thought.* New York: Harper and Brothers, 1943.

Day, Henry C., S. J. *The New Morality.* London: Heath, Cranton, Limited, 1924.

Debo, Angie. *Prairie City.* New York: Alfred A. Knopf, 1944.

Dennett, Mary W. *Birth Control Laws.* New York: F. H. Hitchcock, 1926.

Doyle, Charles Hugo. *Cana is Forever.* New York: Nugent Press, 1949.

Epstein, Ralph C. *The Automobile Industry.* Chicago: Ginn and Co., 1928.

Faulkner, Harold U. *From Versailles to the New Deal.* New Haven: Yale University Press, 1950.

———. *Quest for Social Justice,* 1898-1914. New York: Macmillan Co., 1931.

Furfey, Paul H. *History of Social Thought.* New York: Macmillan Co., 1942.

Gabriel, Ralph H. *The Course of American Democratic Thought.* New York: Ronald Press, 1940.

Hall, T. C. *The Religious Background of American Culture.* Boston: Little Brown & Co., 1930.

High, Stanley. *The Revolt of Youth.* New York: Abingdon Press, 1923.

Howard, John T. *Our American Music.* New York: Crowell Co., 1939.

Irion, F. C. *Public Opinion and Propaganda.* New York: Crowell Co., 1950.

Jacobs, Lewis. *The Rise of the American Film.* New York: Harcourt, Brace and Co., 1937.

Lasswell, Harold D., Casey, Ralph D., Bruce L. *Propaganda and Promotional Activities.* Minnesota: 1935.

Lee, James M. *History of American Journalism.* Chicago: Ginn and Co., 1933.

Lippmann, Walter. *The Phantom Public.* New York: 1925.

———. *Public Opinion.* New York: 1922.

Lindsey, B. B., and Evans, Wainright. *The Companionate Marriage.* New York: 1929.

Lydgate, William A. *What America Thinks.* New York: 1944.

Lynd, Robert S., and Helen M. *Middletown.* New York: Harcourt, Brace and Co., 1929.

Moore, E. R. *The Case Against Birth Control.* New York: Century Co., 1931.

Morris, L. *Postscript to Yesterday.* New York: Random House, 1947.

Mott, Frank L. *American Journalism: A History of Newspapers in the United States.* New York: Macmillan Co., 1941.

Mott, George Fox (ed.). *New Survey of Journalism.* New York: Barnes & Noble, Inc., 1950.

Myers, G. *History of Bigotry in the United States.* New York: Random House, 1943.

Oberholtzer, E. P. *The Morals of the Movies.* Philadelphia: Pen Publishing Co., 1923.

Odegard, Peter. *The American Public Mind.* New York: 1930.

Parkes, H. B. *Recent America: The United States Since 1900.* New York: Crowell Co., 1941.

Parrington, Vernon J. *Main Currents in American Thought.* 3 vols. New York: Harcourt, Brace and Co., 1930.

Pierce, Bessie L. *Public Opinion and the Teaching of History in the United States.* New York: 1926.

Pius XI. *Casti Connubii.* Discussion Club Outline, New York: Paulist Press, 1941.

Robinson, Henry M. *Fantastic Interim.* New York: Harcourt, Brace and Co., 1943.

Rogers, Agnes, and Allen, Frederick Lewis. *I Remember Distinctly.* New York: Harper and Brothers, 1947.

Salmon, Lucy M. *The Newspaper and Authority.* New York: Oxford University Press, 1923.

————. *The Newspaper and the Historian.* New York: Oxford University Press, 1923.

Scott, James R. A. *Influence of the Press.* New York: 1931.

Schrieftgiesser, Karl. *This Was Normalcy.* Boston: Little Brown and Co., 1948.

Seltzer, Laurance H. *A Financial History of the American Automobile Industry.* Boston: Houghton Mifflin Co., 1928.

Slosson, Preston William. *The Great Crusade and After, 1914-1928.* New York: Macmillan Co., 1930.

Soule, George. *Prosperity Decade.* New York: Rinehart and Co., Inc., 1947.

Sullivan, Mark. *Our Times 1900-1925.* Vol. VI. New York: Charles Scribner's Sons, 1935.

Sweet, W. W. *The Story of Religion in America.* New York: Harper and Brothers, 1943.

Weaver, R. B. *Amusements and Sports in American Life.* Chicago: University of Chicago Press, 1939.

Wish, Harvey. *Contemporary America: The National Scene Since 1900.* New York: Harper Brothers, 1948.

Yearbooks

Cahen, Alfred (ed.). *Statistical Analysis of American Divorce.* 1932.

Gilette, J. M. "Family Life," *American Year Book.* 1925.

Hansen, H. (ed.). National Automobile Chamber of Commerce. *Facts and Figures of the Automobile Industry.* 1931.

National Department of Commerce. *Statistical Abstract of the United States for 1925.* Washington, 1926.

President's Committee on Economics. *Recent Economic Changes in the United States.* 1929.

Periodicals

Andrews, F. E. "The Mills of Marriage," *North American Review,* CCXVIII (July, 1929), 17-23.

Anon., *Canadian Baptist.* IX (July 13, 1920), 123.

————. New Palestine, III (July 14, 1922), 34.

————. New Palestine, III (August 11, 1922), 97.

————. "The Professor's Football Kick," *Literary Digest,* LXXXIX (May 15, 1926), 31.

————. "When Our Fathers were Wicked Youth," *Literary Digest,* CIII (November 23, 1929), 24.

Dennett, Mary W. "Birth Control and the Episcopalians," *Nation,* CXV (September 27, 1922), 308.

Farnham, Dr. Marynia. "The Tragic Failure of America's Women," *Coronet,* XXII (September, 1947), 3-9.

Feld, Rose. "The Cosmetic Urge," *Collier's,* LXXIX (March 12, 1927), 22.

Hiat, W. S. "Billions Just for Fun," *Collier's,* LXXIV (October 25, 1924), 19, 31.

Miller, L. M. "Margaret Sanger: Mother of Planned Parenthood," *Reader's Digest,* LIX (July, 1951), 27-31.

Rice, G. "The Real All-American," *Collier's,* LXXVIII (November 20, 1926), 16.

White, Percival. "Figuring Us Out," *North American Review,* CCXXVII (January, 1929), 61-71.

Index

A

Aeschylus, 11
Agamemnon, 11
Aldrich, T. B., 165
America (*see* 193, 194); (*see also* Appendix B, 174)
American Birth Control League, The, 143, 149
American Hebrew, The, (*see* 194); (*see also* Appendix B, 176)
Anderson, Charles A., (*see* Appendix B, 176)
Anthony, Saint, 156
As You Like It, 129
Austen, Jane, 33
Automobiles, 14, 47-54, 168-169
  accidents, 49-51, 52
  advent of, 47
  crime, 48, 52, 53
  factor in industrial expansion, 30, 47
  influence on American life, 47, 53
  intoxication, 49
  morals, 48, 50, 52, 53
  opinion of—
    Baptists, 48-50
    Episcopalians, 50
    Lutherans, 51-52
    Methodists, 52-53
    Presbyterians, 54
    Reform Jews, 50
    Roman Catholics, 50-51
    Unitarians, 53-54
  speed of, 49-54

B

"Babe" Ruth, 58
Banquo, 162
Baptism, "Freak," (*see* "Spectacular, The")

Baptist, The, (*see* 194, 195); (*see also* Appendix B, 174)
Baptists, 19 (*see* Appendix B, 174)
  opinion of—
    automobile, 48-50
    baseball, 58
    birth control, 148-149
    companionate marriage, 138
    cosmetics, 94
    crime, 120-121
    dancing, 82-84
    divorce, 154, 160-161
    drug addiction, 124
    fashions, 92, 93
    flagpole-sitting, 67-68
    jazz, 84
    marathons, 71
    motion pictures, 109-111
    prize fighting, 63-64
    smoking, 98
    socio-cultural aspects of the decade, 43-44
    sports, 54-55
    student suicide, 127
    "stunt" flights, 69
Baseball (*see* Sports)
Basketball (*see* Sports)
Bathing Beauty Contest (*see* "Spectacular, The")
Beethoven, Ludwig, 150
Birth Control, 143-150, 168
  American Birth Control League, 143, 149
  Casti Connubii, 150
  Committee on Marriage and the Home of the Federal Council of Churches, 150
  contraception, 143
  Family Limitation, 143

209